Supply Chain Management for Competitive Advantage

By Ade Asefeso MCIPS MBA

Second Edition

ISBN-13: 978-1499757576

ISBN-10: 1499757573

Publisher: AA Global Sourcing Ltd
Website: http://www.aaglobalsourcing.com

Table of Contents

4

Disclaimer

Dedication

To my family and friends who seems to have been sent here to teach me something about who I am supposed to be. They have nurtured me, challenged me, and even opposed me.... But at every juncture has taught me!

This book is dedicated to my lovely boys, Thomas, Michael and Karl. Teaching them to manage their finance will give them the lives they deserve. They have taught me more about life, presence, and energy management than anything I have done in my life.

Chapter 1: Introduction

What is Supply Chain?

Supply chain comprise of all the businesses and individual contributors involved in creating a product, from raw materials to finished merchandise. Examples of supply chain activities include farming, refining, design, manufacturing, packaging and transportation.

Retail companies become involved in supply chain management in order to control product quality, inventory levels, timing, and expenses. In a global economy, supply chain management often includes dealings with companies and individual contributors in other countries, which requires involvement in politics, trade and tariff laws, quality control, and international relationships.

An example of how U.S. retail industry companies are involved with supply chain management was demonstrated by Wal-Mart when it announced its plans for developing a sustainability system for the products sold in its stores, and environmental accountability from all parties involved in its supply chain.

Wal-Mart's Sustainability Index and Supply Chain Green Standards

An example of what happens when the supply chain is neglected or mismanaged was the global toy recall by Mattel in 2007. After it was discovered that some toys manufactured in China contained toxic lead paint and a design flaw which caused a safety hazard, Mattel had to recall 20 million toys that had been distributed and sold around the world.

If your company makes a product from parts purchased from suppliers, and those products are sold to customers, then you have a supply chain. Some supply chains are simple, while others are rather complicated. The complexity of the supply chain will vary with the size of the business and the intricacy and numbers of items that are manufactured.

Elements of the Supply Chain

A simple supply chain is made up of several elements that are linked by the movement of products along it. The supply chain starts and ends with the customer.

Customer: The customer starts the chain of events when they decide to purchase a product that has been offered for sale by a company. The customer contacts the sales department of the company, which enters the sales order for a specific quantity to be delivered on a specific date. If the product has to be manufactured, the sales order will include a requirement that needs to be fulfilled by the production facility.

Planning: The requirement triggered by the customer's sales order will be combined with other orders. The planning department will create a production plan to produce the products to fulfil the customer's orders. To manufacture the products the company will then have to purchase the raw materials needed.

Purchasing: The purchasing department receives a list of raw materials and services required by the production department to complete the customer's orders. The purchasing department sends purchase orders to selected suppliers to deliver the necessary raw materials to the manufacturing site on the required date.

Inventory: The raw materials are received from the suppliers, checked for quality and accuracy and moved into the warehouse. The supplier will then send an invoice to the company for the items they delivered. The raw materials are stored until they are required by the production department.

Production: Based on a production plan, the raw materials are moved to the production area. The finished products ordered by the customer are manufactured using the raw materials purchased from suppliers. After the items have been completed and tested, they are stored back in the warehouse prior to delivery to the customer.

Transportation: When the finished product arrives in the warehouse, the shipping department determines the most efficient method to ship the products so that they are delivered on or before the date specified by the customer. When the goods are received by the customer, the company will send an invoice for the delivered products.

Chapter 2: Origin of Supply Chain Management

A business entity, in the earlier 1950s revolved more around its own self. Merger and acquisitions though prevalent, a firm used to engage its resources for all the activities needed from buying raw materials to manufacturing and then distributing the products to stockists, dealers and retailers. The aim was to produce more, reduce cost, sell more and increase profit, all by oneself. Creating partnerships with upstream or downstream players was not considered. As a result, keeping large inventories on the shop floor to sustain mass production was considered necessary. However, as the competition grew in 1970s the need for cost reduction got greatly emphasized and soon there were efforts to reduce inventory. Material requirement planning (MRP) and Manufacturing Resource planning (MRP II) systems were introduced to reduce inventory holding.

Need for effective Materials management was duly recognized. The advancement in Information Technology, witnessing application of complicated software for tracking and managing inventories through LAN and WAN became competitive factors. Concepts such as JIT and TQM helped the processing on the shop floor. The origin of supply chain management can be traced to 80s.

The 80s saw a dramatic change in the business scenario all over the world due to globalization and liberalization. Low cost, high quality product and customer delight became the buzz words for the industry. Increased dependence on JIT and TQM methodologies created the vision for strategic partnerships. Development in IT further reduced the national boundary concepts. The first mention of the term supply chain management was found in a paper published in 1982 in the US.

Market globalization also presented a great opportunity to reach out to high potential global markets. This needed relook of the way inventory and logistics were being done.

The challenges associated with enhancement in quality, manufacturing efficiency, customer service and new product design and development also increased.

To deal with these challenges, manufacturers began buying from a select number of certified, high quality suppliers with excellent service reputations and involved these suppliers in their new product design and development activities as well as in cost, quality and service improvement initiatives.

Obviously, supplier management and customer management became focused activities for a firm and Supply Chain Management became popular as a source of competitive advantage for the firms.

Today, Supply Chain Management has concretized for itself into the purchasing and supply management emphasis from industrial buyers and the transportation and logistics emphasis from the wholesalers and the retailers. The new well talked about concepts are supply chain spanning from the supplier's supplier on the one hand to the customer's customer on the other hand.

In the future, it is expected that supply chain management emphasis will concentrate on supply chain expansion, increasing supply chain responsiveness and further reducing supply chain costs.

Importance of Supply Chain Management - SCM, a set of critically important functions

When we talk about the importance of Supply chain management we try to bring into sharp focus the loss due to the absence of an effective supply chain strategy and or the benefit due to a well oiled supply chain for any firm. Basically, it is a question of how good is the integration of supply chain that matters for any firm.

Of critical importance in today's business scenario is managing competition through partners

An independent firm on its own may not have all the resources to match its competitors. But by having an upstream and a downstream arrangement of getting the input, processing it into output and then pushing it to the downstream for distribution with effective chain partners it can face any business challenges.

Importance of having a robust Supply Chain Management can be understood by an example:

BC manufactures the cycle chains for a cycle manufacturing company XY. Another company PQ manufactures bits used in the cycle chain manufactured by BC. In coming days, as per the market forecast, XY shall need 150,000 units of cycle chain, an information that is not available with BC. Accordingly, PQ also does not know how many bits to produce in order to meet BC's requirement. The result would be either both BC and PQ hold high safety stock inventory or lose business respectively with XY and BC.

Now, if in this example showing only three supply chain partners, absence of a critical information among the partners, that is of production forecast at XY firm results into either a higher inventory level or loss of future business what would happen if the supply chain consisted of a large number of partners, a scenario normally existing for medium to large sized companies, the world over?

In an era of gaining competitive advantage through reduced inventories all over, a company is going to have terrible disadvantage of having to carry unnecessary inventory for the fear of losing future business.

Chapter 3: Supply Chain Management Process

To ensure that the supply chain is operating as efficient as possible and generating the highest level of customer satisfaction at the lowest cost, companies have to adopt Supply Chain Management processes and associated technology. Supply Chain Management has three levels of activities that different parts of the company will focus on; strategic; tactical; and operational.

Strategic

At this level, company management will be looking to high level strategic decisions concerning the whole organization, such as the size and location of manufacturing sites, partnerships with suppliers, products to be manufactured and sales markets.

Tactical

Tactical decisions focus on adopting measures that will produce cost benefits such as using industry best practices, developing a purchasing strategy with favoured suppliers, working with logistics companies to develop cost effect transportation and developing warehouse strategies to reduce the cost of storing inventory.

Operational

Decisions at this level are made each day in businesses that affect how the products move along the supply chain. Operational decisions involve making schedule changes to production, purchasing agreements with suppliers, taking orders from customers and moving products in the warehouse.

Supply Chain Management Technology
If a company expects to achieve benefits from their supply chain management process, they will require some level of investment in technology. The backbone for many large companies has been the vastly expensive Enterprise Resource Planning (ERP) suites. These enterprise software implementations will encompass a company's entire supply chain, from purchasing of raw materials to warranty service of items sold. The complexity of these applications does require a significant cost, not only a monetary cost, but the time and resources required to successfully implement an enterprise wide solution. Buy-in by senior management and adequate training of personnel is key to the success of the implementation. There are now many ERP solutions to choose from and it is important to select one which fits the overall needs of a company's supply chain.

Since the wide adoption of Internet technologies, all businesses can take advantage of Web-based software and Internet communications. Instant communication between vendors and customers allows for timely updates of information, which is key in management of the supply chain.

Chapter 4: Strategic Supply Chain Management

As stated in the previous chapter; Supply chain management operates at three levels; strategic, tactical and operational. At the strategic level, company management makes high level strategic supply chain decisions that are relevant to whole organization. The decisions that are made with regards to the supply chain should reflect the overall corporate strategy that the organization is following.

The strategic supply chain processes that management has to decide upon will cover the breadth of the supply chain. These include product development, customers, manufacturing, vendors and logistics.

Product Development

Senior Management has to define a strategic direction when considering the products that the company should manufacture and offer to their customers. As product cycles mature or products sales decline, management has to make strategic decisions to develop and introduce new versions of existing products into the marketplace, rationalize the current product offering or whether develop a new range of products and services. These strategic decisions may include the need to acquire another company or sell existing businesses. However, when making these strategic product development decisions, the overall objectives of the firm should be the determining factor.

Customers

At the strategic level, a company has to identify the customers for its products and services. When company management makes strategic decisions on the products to manufacture, they need to then identify the key customer segments where company marketing and advertising will be targeted.

Manufacturing

At the strategic level, manufacturing decisions define the manufacturing infrastructure and technology that is required. Based on high level forecasting and sales estimates, the company management has to make strategic decisions on how products will be manufactured. The decisions can require new manufacturing facilities to be built or to increase production at existing facilities. However, if the overall company objectives include moving manufacturing overseas, then the decisions may lean towards using subcontracting and third party logistics. As environmental issues influence corporate policy to a greater extent, this may influence strategic supply chain decisions with regards to manufacturing.

Suppliers

Company management has to decide on the strategic supply chain policies with regards to suppliers. Reducing the purchasing spends for a company can directly relate to an increase in profit and strategically there are a number of decisions that can be made to obtain that result. Leveraging the total company's purchases over many businesses can allow company management to select strategic global suppliers who offer the greatest discounts. But these decisions have to correspond with the overall company objectives. If a company has adopted policies on quality, then strategic decisions on suppliers will have to fall within the overall company objective.

Logistics

As well as strategic decisions on manufacturing locations, the logistics function is key to the success of the supply chain. Order fulfilment is an important part of the supply chain and company management need to make strategic decisions on the logistics network. The design and operation of the network has a significant influence on the performance of the supply chain. Strategic decisions are required on warehouses, distribution centres which transportation modes should be used. If the overall company objectives identify the use of more third party subcontracting, the company may strategically decide to use third party logistics companies in the supply chain.

Strategic decisions determine the overall direction of company's supply chain. They should be made in conjunction with the company's overall objectives and not biased towards any particular product or regional location. These high level decisions can be refined, as required, to the specific needs of the company at the lower levels which allow for tactical and operational supply chain decisions to be made.

Chapter 5: Tactical Supply Chain Management

Tactical supply chain decisions focus on adopting measures that will produce cost benefits for a company. Tactical decisions are made within the constraints of the overarching strategic supply chain decisions made by company management.

The strategic supply chain decisions cover the breadth of the supply chain for the entire company. Tactical supply chain decisions take the strategic message and focus on creating real benefits for the company. These can include tactical decisions in manufacturing, logistics, suppliers and product development.
Manufacturing

Strategic decisions may be made by company executives about the number and location of manufacturing sites to be operated. However, it is at a tactical level that decisions are made on how to produce the products at the lowest cost. Tactical decisions may be made as to the adoption of manufacturing methodologies such as kanban or just-in-time. Tactical decisions may be required at a regional level by using technology that is available that reduces material wastage, but cannot be exported to other manufacturing plants.

Logistics

Although strategic company decisions may require an in-house logistics function to be operational, a tactical decision may be required to use a third party logistics company in a region or country where transportation costs are high and cost benefits can be achieved by outsourcing. Similarly in countries where land costs are high, construction of warehousing facilities may be cost prohibitive and despite not following the strategic vision, a tactical decision is made to use public warehousing.

Suppliers

Many companies recognize the cost benefits of using global suppliers and adopt strategic supply chain policies to take advantage. At a tactical level, management has to work within strategic guidelines to identify and negotiate the terms that will realize the greatest cost benefit across the company.

Product Development

Companies make strategic decisions on the product lines they are committed to producing. Tactical decisions have to be made as to the particular products that should be developed. If a company makes a strategic decision to introduce a new line of TV in Europe, the company has to make tactical decisions regarding the specifications of the TV, what countries they will be sold in, the market segment they will targeted and where the most profit can be achieved.

The tactical supply chain decisions that a company makes are not made in isolation but within the framework of the strategic supply chain decisions made at a global level, which in turn are based on the global objectives of the company.

Chapter 6: Operational Supply Chain Management

Operational supply chain decisions are made hundreds of times each day in a company. These are the decisions that are made at business locations that affect how products are developed, sold, moved and manufactured.

Operational decisions are made with awareness of the strategic and tactical decisions that have been adopted within a company. These higher level decisions are made to create a framework within the company's supply chain operate and to the best competitive advantage. The day to day operational supply chain decisions ensure that the products efficiently move along the supply chain achieving the maximum cost benefit. A number of examples of operational decisions can be identified in manufacturing, supplier relationships and logistics.

Manufacturing

Companies make tactical decisions with regards to manufacturing, such as the adoption of kanban and just-in-time. However, if the local manufacturing site is unable to rely on certain supplier's delivery times, the just-in-time method may not be suitable for some product lines. The local plant management may make an operational decision to keep certain items in stock to ensure that production is not halted. This inventory will increase costs, but a greater cost would be incurred if the production line was brought to a standstill due to a lack of items from a supplier.

Suppliers

Global suppliers and negotiated contracts are decisions made at a company level to take advantage of the company's global buying power. This offers considerable cost savings, but local sites may have to make operational decisions with suppliers to ensure an efficient supply chain. In some instances local negotiations with global suppliers are required to ensure quality of the product. For example, in some countries the quality of the product produced by a supplier is not at the same level as other countries. The local management would have to make an operational decision to negotiate with the supplier for them to create a product with a higher quality to ensure the quality of the finished product.

Logistics

Strategic and tactical supply chain decisions in the logistics process often focus on the use of third party logistics companies (3PL). Many companies have identified the cost benefits of these 3PL companies and have integrated them into their supply chain. However, in some instances these 3PL companies may not operate in all regions where the company requires logistics. In those cases the local management has to make operational decisions on leasing local warehousing and negotiating with regional logistics companies.

Although strategic and tactical supply chain decisions are made to bring the greatest efficiencies at the lowest cost, the daily operations of the supply chain require that local management make hundreds of operational decisions. These operational decisions are made within the framework created by the strategic and tactical processes and not made in isolation.

Chapter 7: Lean Supply Chain Management

Lean supply chain management is not exclusively for those companies who manufacture products, but by businesses who want to streamline their processes by eliminating waste and non-value added activities. Companies have a number of areas in their supply chain where waste can be identified as time, costs or inventory. To create a leaner supply chain companies must examine each area of the supply chain.

Procurement

Many businesses have complex procurement operations. Large companies often have corporate procurement groups as well as local procurement. This can lead to vendors being given multiple contracts leading to variations in prices depending on location. Companies that practice lean supply chain management reduce their procurement function so that each vendor has one point of contact, one contract and offers one price for all locations.

Businesses are looking to new technologies to assist them in improving procurement processes. These include internet based purchasing that allows requisitioners to purchase items from vendor's catalogue containing companywide contract prices. Changes in payment options to vendors can also streamline processes. Companies that use a two-way match, which is payment on receipt rather than payment on invoice, will reduce resources in their procurement department as well as improve supplier relationships.

Manufacturing

Lean supply chain management gained popularity in the manufacturing area as this is where significant improvement can be achieved. Manufacturing processes can be improved to reduce waste and resources while maintaining operational performance. Companies who have adopted lean supply chain practices have examined each of their routings, bill of materials and equipment to identify where improvements can be achieved.

Warehousing

Warehouse processes should be examined to find areas of eliminating waste of resources and non-value added steps. One area the companies should always be working on is the reduction of unnecessary inventory. The accumulation of inventory requires resources to store and maintain it. By reducing unnecessary inventory, a company can minimize warehousing space and handling, in turn reducing overall costs.

Transportation

Businesses who want to implement lean processes often look to their transportation procedures to see where they can be streamlined. In many instances companies find that their efforts to improve customer satisfaction leads to poor shipping decisions. Orders are shipped without combining additional orders to minimize costs or expensive shipping options are selected because of a customer request. Businesses often find that they are using a number of shippers unnecessarily when they could be reducing their shipping options and reduce overall costs.

Lean supply chain management requires businesses to examine every process in their supply chain and identify areas that are using unnecessary resources, which can be measured in dollars/pounds, time or raw materials. This will improve the company's competitiveness as well as improve the company's overall profitability.

Chapter 8: Green Supply Chain Best Practices

The trend towards developing a green supply chain is now gaining popularity but most companies are still coming to terms with how this can be achieved and where do they start. For years businesses have been concentrating on improving supply chain visibility, refining efficiency and minimizing cost. Despite the focus being moving towards a green supply chain the goals of visibility, efficiency and cost reduction do not have to be discarded. By examining the companies who have already made strides towards to a green supply chain, we can begin to see some best practices that will help others to begin their own transition.

Align Your Green Supply Chain Goals with Business Goals

Creating a green supply chain that has little to do with your business will not help your company to achieve its business objectives. For example, if a company decides to use biodegradable packaging for its products that costs 25% more than traditional packaging, this goes against the businesses goals of reducing costs. If a business has an overall goal to reduce costs then the move to a green supply chain should fit together with the business goal. A company should look at its overall business goals and identify how a transition to a green supply chain can help achieve those goals. For example if a business wants to reduce its energy costs it should start by looking at the consumption to see if a reduction can be made by using more energy efficient and greener equipment.

Use Green Supply Chain to Improve Processes

Companies do not often change their businesses processes and it is this attitude that allows inefficient processes to continue unabated causing unnecessary waste and pollution. For example ineffective processes in the US automotive industry allowed the innovative Japanese automakers to become market leaders.

Businesses that want to transition to a green supply chain should take the opportunity to review all of their business processes to identify areas where adopting a greener outlook can actually improve their business. Companies should review each process along the supply chain to identify if a more environmentally sound approach will help cure the inefficiencies that occur. Many companies that have been through this exercise have identified processes where raw materials were wasted; resources underutilized and unnecessary energy used due to inefficient equipment.

Green Suppliers and Material Refurbishment

Companies reviewing their business processes should look beyond their factory walls. When reviewing purchasing processes the aim of any company, looking to transition to a green supply chain, should be to find suppliers who have minimized their environmental impact without reducing the quality of their product or significantly raising costs. By purchasing products from green suppliers businesses can then begin their green supply chain before any material reaches their site.

At the opposite end of the supply chain businesses should look at their return process. Many businesses have not developed a successful refurbishment program for their products that have been returned or exchanged. By offering refurbished items businesses can increase purchasing options to their customers and widen their customer base, whilst improving the environmental impact of their products.

There are many ways in which businesses can transition to a green supply chain; however it is important to realize that it is difficult to achieve results without strong focused leadership. Senior management has to lead the effort to move to a green supply chain and provide the resources for the transition. Many businesses have documented intent or plan to implement a green supply chain, but without the necessary resources, both financial and manpower, any impact will be minimal.

Chapter 9: Benchmarking in the Supply Chain

Supply chain operations within an organization should be constantly reviewed to identify where improvements can be made or deficiencies eliminated. One method to help do this is to perform a series of benchmarking tests on their supply chain processes. Benchmarking or goal setting allows a company to assess the opportunities they may have for improving a number of areas in their supply chain including productivity, inventory accuracy, shipping accuracy, storage density and bin-to-bin time. The benchmarking process can provide a company some estimate of the benefits achieved by the implementation of any improvements.

History of Benchmarking

Benchmarking is the process whereby an assessment of an act or performance is measured by some means, whether this is by a measurement of time, value or quantity. For example, an assessment of moving items from one storage location to another can be measured by time for a single movement or by quantity if the performance is over a set period. A benchmarking project will gather the assessments and develop a plan of action to improve the process that was assessed.

The popularity of benchmarking was spearheaded by the Xerox Corporation in the 1980's and is now used in corporations throughout the world.

Types of Benchmarking

Three types of benchmarking can be identified; internal which is focused on the processes of a single company, external which examines processes outside of a company's direct industry and competitive, which examines processes at firms within the same industry.

Internal Benchmarking

The internal benchmarking process allows a company with a number of facilities that operate the same supply chain processes to compare and contrast the ways in which the process is performed in those facilities. For example if a company operates five distribution centres in the UK and France, the benchmarking process can examine a number of operations that take place at each of the distribution centres and compare how they are performed and what improvements can be made by comparing the results of the benchmarking. If a company benchmarks the processes around inventory accuracy, shipping accuracy and storage density, the results of the assessments of the facilities can help a company to improve on those processes at all of the facilities.

External Benchmarking

For companies that have performed internal benchmarking and want to investigate new ways in which to improve performance of their internal processes, external benchmarking can produce significant improvements. Many companies believe that their processes are as efficient as possible, but quite often, the efficiencies are limited by the knowledge within the company. The external benchmarking process takes a company outside of its own industry and exposes them to different methods and procedures. For example, a manufacturer and distributor of electrical components have internally benchmarked their warehouses for a number of years and have exhausted ideas on improving efficiencies. They approached a very successful retail company to visit their central warehouse and benchmark the processes that occur there to compare to their own warehouse processes. The external benchmarking allowed the manufacturer of the electrical components to assess the processes seen in the retailer's warehouse and develop an improvement plan for their own facilities based on the results.

Competitive Benchmarking

For companies that are not performing as well as their competitors they may want to identify the reasons why their processes are not as efficient. Consulting and research firms can perform competitive benchmarking studies for companies that will identify the strengths and weaknesses of their processes based on those of their competitors. The company can then produce improvement plans based on the results of the competitive benchmarking.

Components of Benchmarking

There are a number of components to a benchmarking study. Not every benchmarking project

41

will incorporate these components, but a combination of these can be used.

1. Financial benchmarking: This involves a financial analysis of the operations that are assessed. For example, a company can compare the cost of storing a component in each of its warehouses.

2. Performance benchmarking: This can compare the efficiency of performing a task in one company location to another, or to a competitor's.

3. Product benchmarking: This method compares the product of one company against another, or comparing between facilities in the same company.

4. Strategic benchmarking: This method observes how other companies compete. This can be within the same industry or outside of the companies industry.

5. Functional benchmarking: This is considered to be traditional benchmarking where a company will benchmark a single process at a location or a number of locations to identify where efficiencies can be made.

Chapter 10: Push or Pull

Push or pull? That is a question every Procurement Manager needs to answer. Before you do, it is important to understand what it means and how it affects the supply chains.

Understanding what it means depends a whole lot on the context. It also changes the question from push or pull to a question of where should the inflection occur.

Depending on the number of links in the extended supply chain, the boundary of push and pull processes can be established. Setting up the boundary at 1 represents a fully pull-based supply chain that illustrates that the planning for a product starts when customer places the order and creates firm demand. Moving this all the way to the last link at 4 represents a full push-based supply chain that illustrates that the products are built, distributed, and ready for the customer demand. There are two other intermediate positions 2 and 3 that are possible. These can represent the intermediate scenarios where the final product may be assembled when the customer order is placed to distribution scenarios where products are ready but distributed or shipped in response to demand.

Analyzing the push/pull decisions in this context generally allows the companies to understand how their extended supply chain works and what might work best for them as a business strategy. Of course, this decision depends on a lot of other factors such as the attributes of the product and demand itself. For example, detergent is not the likeliest candidate for a pull-based scenario and luxury yachts would probably not fit the bill for a push-based scenario. However, understanding the overall supply-chain and analyzing the product and demand characteristics within that context does help companies understand their options and even opens new segments in an industry that may not have existed till then. Dell is a great example where they identified a niche and developed a pull-based industry supply chain for personal computers where none existed prior to that.

Push or Pull in a Single Enterprise Supply Chain:

The same concept, when seen in the context of a single enterprise supply chain, can be understood more as an inventory-order interface. Supply chains are modelled as a series of processes that are connected through inventory buffers. In the case of a conventional brick-and-mortar retailer, the positions 1 and 4 will be impractical -- after all, they must have products physically available in the stores when the customers walk-in. The inventory-order interface at links 2 and 3 will be perfectly valid as the retailer can either choose to replenish their regional warehouses or their distribution centres or both. In that sense, the processes to the left of points 2 and 3 will represent push-based processes and those to the right will be pull-based.

However, in the context of Internet based retail operations, order-inventory interface can move to almost any position. The retailer can choose to fulfil customer orders from the inventories in their own regional warehouses or distribution centres, or, they can choose to fulfil customer orders directly from their suppliers in what is called a drop-ship model.

For supply chains, then the question is not push or pull, but rather where in the supply chain should inflection occur? What is the optimal point where the supply chain changes from a push-based supply chain to a pull-based supply chain. All supply chains must be a combination of push and pull processes; purely push or purely pull supply chains exist only in theory (imagine a purely pull-based supply chain that must start prospecting for minerals to make steel to make automobiles after an order is placed!).

Deciding where the inventory-order point must be placed is a matter of analyzing much more than just the supply chain operations. The products, market conditions, demand patterns, competitive and other external market pressures must be understood and analyzed to make such a decision. The decision affects the operational costs, response times to fulfil demand, agility (ability to react to changes in demand), as well as flexibility (ability to react to changes in product design or demand location, for example). There are no standard templates, but there are some helpful matrices using the product and demand patterns that aid this decision.

Chapter 11: Business Strategy and Supply Chains

What do supply chains have to offer to the business strategy? It turns out, a lot.

To understand, let us review some of the basic concepts of strategy. Strategy was initially postulated as a balancing act between the external and internal forces in a corporation where the firm matched its (internal) strengths and weaknesses against the (external) opportunities and threats. Since then, many researchers have added their own work to the field of defining what is corporate strategy, how to think about it, how to formulate good strategy, and have provided various frameworks to help the evolution of the concept of corporate strategy. In short, the goal of any corporate strategy is to create competitive advantages for the business in its industry segment so that it is well-positioned for financial success.

Porter's three generic strategies

Porter's three basic strategies were suggested by him in 90s and have become a mainstay of the strategy literature. These three strategies are based on pursuing cost, differentiation, or focus as the main strategy and then adopting the policies, investments, and projects around that.

The cost strategy is based on pursuing the cost leadership so that the firm has a definite cost advantage over the competition. If the firm is successful in achieving cost that is below the average cost of products/services offered in a segment, then it allows the firm to either be more profitable or expand its market share.

Differentiation strategy postulates that firms can have competitive advantages over the others in their segment if they can image develop unique features in their products or services that are valuable to its customers. Of course, for this strategy to work, the cost of developing these unique features must be less than the premium that the buyers are ready to pay for these features.

The third generic strategy is the focus strategy that primary postulates creating a niche within the segment to achieve competitive advantage. These niches are created when the product is specifically designed and targeted at a well defined customer segment. The firm must identify the customer segment it wants to target and then define the unique features that will be valuable to this segment; note that cost itself may be one of those unique features that appeal to this segment, so can be other product features. There are many styles of strategies now defined that are primarily combinations and variations of these three generic strategies. That makes sense because a company may adopt different strategies for different business units or products depending on its current positioning in that segment, its strengths, available resources, and skills required to address the demands of a strategy.

Resource based view of strategy

A Resource-based View (RBV) of the competitive advantages emerged on the premise that it is only the resources of a firm that create the competitive advantages. When a firm possesses resources that are unique to it and can create value for its buyers, then the firm has competitive advantages. These resources can be direct such as cash and assets, indirect such as brand value, or firm's capabilities such as its supply chain processes.

Capability based view of strategy

Then, there is the concept of competing on capabilities. This became a prevalent way of thinking about strategy for example Wal-mart capabilities won the company the top spot in its industry segment.

It is a little ironic that capabilities came last in the evolution of thinking on corporate strategy since this is so basic to the success of corporations as well as to the successful implementation of any strategy the firm may have picked up to pursue. After all, any strategy that remains unexecuted does not deliver. Executing a strategy necessarily means that firms create capabilities that are demanded by the strategy. Take, for example, the cost strategy that Wal-mart has followed since its inception; is the capabilities that Wal-mart developed to pursue the low-cost strategy that allowed it to reduce costs across its value chain. If Wal-mart was unable to create and maintain such functional capabilities then simply having a strategy to pursue low costs does not do any good. To pursue low cost, Wal-mart analyzed its whole value chain and developed capabilities in all business functions where such potential existed; such as store operations, distribution, warehousing, inventory management, and even merchandising functions such as seasonal merchandise and pricing optimization.

The same remains true for any other strategy that a firm might select. For example, differentiation strategy may lead to developing capabilities in product design, manufacturing, delivery, or customer service. Consider Kindle: this is a clear example that has propelled Amazon to develop capabilities in innovative product design which was not its mainstay as a retailer! Also consider the delivery model of the books using Kindle that provides another clear differentiator to Amazon compared to its competitors.

While the resource strategy considers direct and indirect resources as enabling competitive advantages and that is true, the fact is that these resources themselves are a result of functional capabilities that, over time, have delivered these resources in addition to their direct contribution to creating the competitive advantages. If Coke as a brand is valuable today, it is because the company developed superior marketing capabilities in the past years that have consistently worked towards creating the brand that now can be leveraged as a competitive advantage. Same is true for cash assets that Wal-mart may have; these assets themselves are a result of their functional capabilities allowing cost reduction rather than the other way around. Therefore, I see the direct and indirect resources simply as by-products of a successful strategy that drives functional capabilities to create competitive advantages and also delivers these benefits in terms of direct/indirect resources which can be leveraged in advancing these competitive advantages. Remember that these resources alone are not sustainable by themselves and continue to depend on the original functional capabilities that created them in the first place.

The capabilities based competitive advantages, therefore, just happens to be the core precept of creating and maintaining strategic edge in an industry.

Now that we have refreshed the basic concepts of strategy, let us see what can supply chains offer to corporate strategy?

Supply chains primarily focus on the operations of a firm; supply chain council defines the five basic supply chain functions as Plan, Source, Make, Deliver, and Return. Depending on the industry you are in, all or some of these functions will be part of your supply chain. All the supply chain functions primarily offer the firm cost reduction opportunities directly or indirectly. Supply chain functions like warehouse automation and transportation optimization direct reduce their cost of goods sold (COGS), and other functions like inventory optimization reduce the requirements for working capital thus increasing return on assets (ROA). All these options provide opportunities for creating competitive advantages for a firm.

Then, there are other supply chain functions that can provide differentiators through process integration, such as those in the order fulfilment area. These functions not only add to the operational efficiency but can also provide differentiation in customer service through perfect order fulfilment and ability to track and communicate the customer order status throughout the fulfilment process.

Better planning through better demand forecasting can affect all the operations in a supply chain in a made-to-stock or retail situations. These planning functions can substantially reduce the cost basis by reducing inventory, increasing manufacturing operations efficiency, increasing distribution operations efficiency, and in reducing plan volatility that stabilizes the operations.

Optimization based supply chain solutions such as manufacturing planning, scheduling, and sequencing; inventory optimization, transportation optimization, purchase planning, etc. make use of powerful mathematical models to represent the real-life supply chain constraints with the objective of reducing cost or increasing throughput. Both of these (reducing cost or increasing throughput) can help organizations create and sustain competitive advantages by creating cost, delivery, and customer service differentiators.

Firms should analyze their corporate strategies and dissect their value chain (operations) to establish the functional capabilities that will help them achieve the goals set by such strategies. Supply chain functions, specifically, provide many such opportunities and combined with standard packages solutions can help the companies achieve their strategic goals systematically when these efforts are aligned with the strategic goals through the identification of required functional capabilities.

Chapter 12: Functional Strategy and Supply Chains

Business strategy alone can direct, but does not deliver. It can set the direction, provide objectives, specify the desired corporate goals, but does not take you there. That important step is left to the strategy execution. What does that consist of; converting the business strategy into the functional and deployment strategies, and converting them further down to individual plans and projects that can be executed. If each of the functional strategies are aligned with the business strategy and support the goals set by the business strategy, then it becomes a powerful roadmap for achieving the desired results. The rest of the discussion deals with the functional and deployment level strategy and execution, and tries to establish the correlation and the need for alignment among these three levels of strategies.

I am using the words "functional strategy" to emphasize the fact that functional capabilities provide functional competencies that allow the corporations to achieve their strategic goals, as well as establish competitive advantage in most cases. This is also the premise of competitive advantage that Porter talks about in his strategy discussions. The "deployment strategy" is primarily a reference to technology strategy since technology has become the de-facto enabler for the business processes, and it directly affects the cost of creating, enhancing and maintaining such capabilities. This (enabling technology) is generally seen as a support activity in conventional strategy literature, but the acute dependence on technology for day-to-day operations has changed the way companies must plan for technology today.

Functional strategies most important to a retailer would be the strategies for supply chain, merchandising, and store operations. Depending on the business of the corporation, this focus may change. In retail or manufacturing industries, supply chains will remain a huge focus area for developing process competency through strategy planning, as a very large part of the corporate operations fall within the scope of supply chain management processes. Ensuring that the supply chain strategy is aligned with the business strategy not only helps reach these goals, but also provides an objective method for prioritizing the supply chain initiatives within other organizational and functional constraints. An example of such organizational constraint can be the available funds that must be spread across all functional initiatives including the supply chain. An example of a functional constraint can be the unavailability of consistent item master data across various stores that may then constrain the ability to correctly plan for the optimal inventory across the enterprise. A functional strategy defines the guidelines for the prioritization of functional areas where the development of organizational competence will get the biggest rewards.

Consider a retailer whose business strategy revolves around providing value pricing. This strategy can be achieved through merchandising functions by changing assortments to cheaper products that functionally serve the same utilitarian function as a more expensive product, or by creating store brands where costs are closely controlled by the retailer. The same strategy can also be achieved through improving supply chain functions that reduce the cost of operations like better inventory planning, transportation optimization, cross-docking; by having a lower cost basis, the savings can then be passed on as value based pricing. The strategy objectives can also be reached through enhanced store operations like better labour planning, reducing floor associates through installation of price checking stations, product finder stations, and self-service POS lanes; again the savings can be passed to the customers in the form of value based pricing.

Which one of the above is the best course of action? This question can only be answered by rising above individual functions and considering all of the following:

1. What is the target for value based pricing? How much difference does the retailer wish to maintain with the competition?
2. Is changing assortment for pursuing the value based pricing even feasible? This could be true for commodity items, but not where consumers value the brands.
3. What is the potential of each strategy for providing the value based pricing, which one provides the largest profitability potential?
4. What is the cost and time for implementation of each of the functional strategies?

5. What other benefits each of the strategies provide? As none of these solutions work in isolation, they do have other consequences as well. For example, reducing knowledgeable store associates does affect customer service negatively.
6. What strategies produce synergies with other corporate goals? For example, improving demand and inventory planning may also support more flexibility in refreshing assortments more frequently.

A functional strategy establishes the direction for creating, enhancing, and maintaining the functional competence within the functional area. Such a strategy will not only support the business strategy, but may also provide options to consider that may not be available in absence of a specific functional competence. For example, once the competitive price collection and analysis capability is established as part of the functional strategy execution, then value based pricing may have another option of defining store specific value pricing using the regional competitive data, rather than having a chain-wide pricing strategy. Both way, the functional strategies establish the direction for the evolution of functional competence, and a functional strategy that is fully aligned with the business strategy is always most desirable.

As almost all functional processes are enabled and supported by technology, having a technology strategy that is aligned with the business and functional strategies is equally necessary. Technology strategy is driven by the business strategy, but in turn, it also drives the business strategy. For example, a business strategy for developing inventory planning capabilities drives the technology solution to be pursued, but the technology pursued may drive the need for establishing common master data across enterprise divisions to effectively deliver the inventory planning capabilities. This introduces another level of complexity in aligning the three strategies and prioritizing the investments. I call this a "process sequencing constraint" where a process capability cannot be developed without first developing another process capability. These constraints can be soft when they can be worked around or hard when they cannot be worked around. In the above example, having a common item master is desirable, but by developing an interim solution for mapping several divisional item masters, the problem can be solved to an extent. However, if the functional strategy wanted to pursue transportation optimization, but master data on the shipping attributes of the items/orders was missing, it would almost be a hard constraint. Therefore technology strategy also affects the business strategy as much as it supports it.

In fact, as most of the investments for creating a functional capability remain in technology, it has the potential to become a real constraint, limiting the flexibility of the business, if it has not been thought through, and aligned with the other two.

Technology strategy establishes the direction for the applications (custom, packaged, etc.), information (master data, meta-data, business intelligence, etc.), and technology (hardware, software, vendors, open source, SOA, etc.). These decisions, in turn, affect the cost of deploying functional strategies, as well as the TCO for creating and maintaining the process capabilities and organizational competence.

In summary, it pays to have functional and deployment strategies closely aligned to the business strategy. It provides a roadmap for organizational evolutions, as well as a practical tool for prioritization of spend on developing process competencies mandated by the business strategy.

Chapter 13: Do it Right

This chapter is about some of the factors that corporations must ensure in order to fully leverage their supply chain solutions and the promised returns on their investments.

People:

Supply chain planning solutions typically are built as decision support systems with complex algorithms underneath. These solutions require people with the right skills for configuration, tuning, reviewing and resolving errors, and maintaining the planning parameters for the system to function at its best. Depending on the solution, these skills may vary from statistics, to mathematical programming, to data mining, etc. People can acquire these skills through training, academic background, and/or prior professional experience. However, the key is to plan for the people with right skills and not undermine the solution capabilities for want of a few good people. Also remember that we are talking about only a handful of super users that would fall in this category, since the large majority of the users, using the output of such systems don't have to be specialists at all.

Process:

Most corporations believe that their processes are unique, and therefore provide them with competitive advantage that others in the same industry do not have. The truth is that for most part, it is a myth.

Very few processes in an enterprise actually have the potential of providing such competitive advantage, while most others will be just fine as long as they are efficiently planned, executed, and reviewed. Being open to review the old processes in an unbiased way, and adopting the standard process supported by the solution not only shortens the implementation timelines, it also saves money, and resources. And usually, it provides a standard way of doing business with other partners in the industry using similar solutions. Be open to evaluate all processes and adopt changes where such changes make sense.

Infrastructure:

Successfully implementing complex business applications requires proper infrastructure planning. With infrastructure in this context, I mean hardware as well as software infrastructure. An example of software infrastructure will be ability to manage common master data among many business applications; ability to extract, cleanse, consolidate, govern, and publish such data to all applications that need them; ability to analyze information; ability to collaborate; have automated alerts, and event based messaging to prompt user action when required. Often these capabilities are not planned as part of the supply chain solutions since they are not mandatory. However, they allow the enterprise to fully leverage the core solution while absence of these capabilities truly constrains the ability to reap any substantial ROI. To a large extent, this can also be said about the hardware; having centrally hosted servers with proper back-up, disaster recovery plans that are routinely tested, high speed network among corporate locations, RF terminals, large monitors, etc., does add to the overall productivity, usability, and adoption of these applications. Only such investments with the right processes ensure business continuity in natural or man-made disasters. Having the correct infrastructure for a supply chain technology initiative requires holistic planning, the kind that is mostly missing from IT-centric project planning exercises.

Customization:

This is another huge factor affecting successful implementation and adoption of new supply chain solutions. Unless a solution is custom built to your requirements, chances are that your processes will never map a 100% to the process supported by the packaged solution. However, to avoid functionality gaps that may be truly constraining, you must determine these gaps prior to the investment in the solution. Since most of the bigger software vendors would have years of experience with similar customers, it is also a good opportunity to question all such gaps and determine if they are real gaps, or merely entrenched habits that are hard to break. Remember, every custom enhancement to the solution costs money to develop, pushes back the project timelines affecting ROI, becomes a permanent constraint to solution upgrades, increases on-going maintenance fees, and adds to testing and validation costs for original deployment and every upgrade thereafter. This is a sure project killer.

Metrics:

What gets measured gets delivered. Therefore, define clear expectations on prospective operational improvements through well-defined metrics. What is it that the technology is expected to deliver: higher inventory turns, higher number of orders processed per buyer, higher fulfilment rates? Also make sure that you have the historical data on these metrics to compare the new numbers against. All ROI is questionable unless it can be established through consistent trend on the defined metrics, against a historical data set. Finally, make sure that these new metrics are aligned with the people's individual goals. Many a times, personnel goals are tied to the operational metrics, and when these operational metrics get revised due to new technology, the revision of the personnel goals is easily forgotten. But remembering to realign the two will make sure people have no hesitation in adopting the new technology, since the new technology is going to help them with their new set of goals.

Chapter 14: Retail vs. Manufacturing

At a high level, supply chains address the same needs for all companies, managing the flow of goods and services in an optimal fashion. However the core supply chain competencies change based on the industry vertical. Understanding these differences enhances a corporation's ability to leverage their supply chain assets and solutions effectively. Here is a quick summary of such competencies for retail and manufacturing environments.

Investment/Assets:

For Retail, the primary investment is in the merchandise flowing through its network, at rest or in motion. (We exclude any real estate assets from this discussion as these are not core to supply chain operations. Whether a retail company owns the stores, or leases them, does not impact its operations substantially). Therefore managing this asset (inventory in the network) becomes core to a Retailer's success. That is why the Retail supply chains are distribution focused. After the cost of merchandise, the largest overheads in retail are related to their stocking and distribution of goods. So much so that GMROI for Retailers is quite commonly interpreted and computed as Gross Margin Return on Inventory (as against Gross Margin Return on Investment). A lean distribution chain means optimal services levels between the supplying and consuming network nodes and a higher inventory turns. The level of inventory directly affects the operational cash-flow and ability to service customers and both these competing needs must be managed effectively.

For Manufacturers, the goods (raw materials as well as finished goods) within the network are a large investment, but another substantial investment is in manufacturing/process equipment, and resources. All equipment gets depreciated over time irrespective of the percentage utilization. However such equipment adds value to a manufacturer's operations only when it is being utilized. Therefore manufacturers must worry about maintaining optimal levels of inventory to maintain the services levels among the supplying and consuming network nodes but also about keeping the equipment and resources effectively utilized. In doing so the focus of the supply chain changes considerably from being distribution focused to being asset focused (though the relative importance of asset utilization over optimal inventory management will be determined by the cost of raw material to finished goods ratio that represents the value added). This introduces the need for manufacturing planning, scheduling and sequencing so that all manufacturing operations as well as transportation operations are optimally planned for best use of resources.

Size of the Network

Another difference that accentuates the different core requirements for the Retail and Manufacturing supply chains is simply the size of the network. A retailer's network typically consists of multiple warehouses, and a large number of retail locations that may run into thousands. A manufacturer on the other hand will normally have only a handful of manufacturing locations and warehouses. Therefore managing the flow of material (merchandise, raw materials, or finished goods) through this network through optimal transportation, and warehouse planning becomes much more important in a retail environment.

Also the sheer number of items dealt within the Retail environments is huge compared to most Manufacturing environments (exceptions exist). This adds a large number of vendor shipping locations to the network making it unwieldy and complex for retailers.

Type of Network

As above, Retailer's network primarily consists of storage locations (such as warehouses) and selling locations (such as stores). A Manufacturer's supply chain network primarily consists of storage locations (warehouses for raw materials, or finished goods), and manufacturing locations (factories). An extended network for both the environments can model the vendor's shipping points as well.

These nodes represent different activities in the supply chain, and therefore present different planning challenges. While the Retail chains typically emphasize managing inventory and service levels, the Manufacturing chains also manage resource planning and usage.

This also affects the service-time length of supply chains. Manufacturing supply chains usually have longer end-to-end lead times (due to manufacturing process lead times) and therefore inherently less flexible to volatility. Retail chains can be nimble if managed and modelled well though the size of these chains tends to make them harder to optimize.

Capacity Constraints

In a Retail chain, the capacity constraints are seldom modelled. Most of the capacity can be modelled as infinite as this capacity is mostly an outsourced service. Relevant capacities in Retail that can potentially constrain the supply planning are the supplier capacities, stocking capacities and transportation capacities. As most retailers have multiple suppliers and merchandise that can be easily substituted, the supplier capacities can be considered unconstrained. Same goes for the transportation capacities, as more carriers can be added on routes where required. That leaves the warehousing storage constraints as the only real constraint, but even these are seldom modelled in Retail chains.

In contrast, the Manufacturing chains are constrained by manufacturing capacity (available resources, time, skills, etc.) and this is a real constraint that must be modelled for feasible planning.

As a result, the Retail supply planning primarily consists of propagating demand through the supply chain tiers largely unconstrained, with only the inventory levels and inventory multiples having been modelled. The latter adequately address the need to maintain the desired service levels.

In contrast, the Manufacturing supply planning consists of propagating demand through the supply chain tiers constrained by the manufacturing/processing capacity (the capacity modelling a composite of required resource, skill, and material) at each node, in addition to the inventory levels and inventory multiples that must be maintained for sustaining the desired service levels.

Collaboration with Partners

In both environments, collaboration with partners can become a true differentiator. However it can provide a substantially higher return in Retail environments than in (most) manufacturing environments. The underlying reasons go back to some of the differences discussed above. In a manufacturing environment, there are quite a few parameters around resource planning that are fully controlled within the corporation's four walls, and these alone can provide a compelling ROI for a supply planning exercise. For retailers the main asset being managed through the supply planning is inventory, and a fully collaborative chain can allow for last minute changes, diversions, and re-balancing of this asset across the network for most optimal demand fulfilment.

Therefore each supply chain opportunity needs to be evaluated based on the industry vertical, company specific requirements/expectations. The technology solutions then follow the requirements and expectation analysis. There are several vendors available for supply chain solutions, and each one brings specific strengths that companies will do well to understand and apply in their specific situations.

Chapter 15: Retailers Top-line Growth to Bottom-line Improvement

The initial years for most retailers are focused on the merchandising functions where the product excitement is the main focus. With hyper-competition and super-thin margins, every new retailer must bring to the table some excitement through products; some amount of differentiation or niche segmentation, simply to get into the game. If the excitement catches on, the retailer is soon on its path to growth.

Consider Toys R Us that brought the niche of having a whole super-store like a big warehouse dedicated entirely to the toys or The Home Depot that brought the builder-like warehouse-store formats to the consumers or the Target that promised "pay less expect more" unlike the Wal-mart that simply promised "always low prices". Each of these retailers had to create a segment and create excitement with their assortment when they started.

During these early years, merchandising rules.

But success has its downside; if the retailer becomes successful, the completion quickly catches up. Differentiation blurs, niche becomes crowded, growth slows, and the top-line levels-off.

That is time when the successful retailers separate themselves from the run-of-the-mill. These are the retailers who understood the other half of the retail story: supply chain management and invested in creating supply chains that would provide with the power to stay and still make money when the product excitement wears off, the differentiators become common-place, and niches are over-crowded.

The splendour of glitzy new products on the store shelf must be supported by the sleek sinew supply chain capabilities. Successful retailers understand the two foundations of retail: merchandising and supply chain. Here is a quick overview of the two most critical retail processes.

Merchandising

Merchandising truly defines retail. It is what makes a retailer unique and provides the "niche". It provides the retailer its "identity". Wal-mart shoppers know they will get lowest prices, and they don't necessarily expect the service or variety. Upscale retailers like Neiman Marcus on the other hand are "identified" more with their chic image and differentiated product offerings.

Merchandising has various sub-functions. It has a financial aspect and an assortment aspect.

Merchandise financial planning process helps the retailer create their plans for revenue targets and the budgets for inventories, margins, promotions, and clearance. Planned targets for sales and inventory are set in this process, so are the budgets for promotions, clearance, and marketing. These plans can be started at the top and trickle down the organization, through regional and product hierarchies. Alternately, the process may support a bottom up planning for this function and then reconcile the top-down numbers with these numbers.

Next the assortment plans are created. Assortment plans match the products with the locations to determine what will be sold where. Assortments may vary from store to store based on demographics, competition, weather, fashions, and new products. These plans typically start with the evaluation of the existing product portfolios and establish the new assortments for the planning period. These assortment plans are then reconciled with the merchandising plans to make sure that the product-assortments are aligned with the budgets and sales projections. These assortment plans are typically available at regional, store cluster, product class and sometimes at item levels.

Further down, the assortment plans then generate the macro and micro space planning. Macro space planning constrains the planning process based on logistics, distribution, and storage constraints in the supply chain. Micro space planning creates planograms that determine the product presentation in the stores, presentation quantities, and other displays.

Merchandise planning is primarily the top-line play for a retailer. This is the most important function in the growth stage for any retailer. Its importance does not diminish for mature retailers, though the strategy for mature companies normally shifts from top-line growth to bottom-line improvement; and therefore, cost control becomes more important than growing the top line. And, that is where supply chain comes in.

Supply Chain

Supply chains enable the retailers to get the right products to the right place at the right time. Supply chain processes extend from demand and supply management to inventories and distribution to the stores. By directly controlling the stocking and distribution operations, these processes establish the cost basis and directly affect the profitability of the retailer.

Efficient supply chains can reduce costs in all areas such as inventories, transportation, and warehousing. After the cost of merchandise, the supply chain costs are the biggest costs for a retailer. Even a small savings on these costs can mean millions of dollars/pounds directly going to the bottom line for most retailers. The good news is that unlike the cost of the merchandise, the supply chain costs are directly controllable by the retailer through better planning, optimization, and execution.

Supply chain processes cover network planning, demand planning, supply planning, logistics, and distribution operations.

Supply chain network planning helps in optimally locating the distribution hubs for stocking and distribution of products to the stores and customers. A well designed network will reduce the replenishment lead-time and the distribution costs of products in the stores.

Demand planning is the science of forecasting future demand that must be replenished at each of the warehouses and stores. The forecasting process uses sales history and other user inputs to model seasonality, planned promotions, expected weather patterns, and price; all of which may affect demand. It produces a sales forecast and considers the existing inventory to determine the actual demand that must be replenished through purchasing new product.

Supply planning processes typically cover sourcing, vendor management, inventory planning, replenishment planning, and purchase management. Sourcing establishes the process for finding and selecting vendors that the corporation will deal with.

There may be supply contracts and relationship guidelines that are part of the process. Vendor management refers to on-going relationship management, and vendor performance evaluation. Inventory planning determines how much to stock to meet a desired service level, at selling locations, and at stocking locations. Replenishment planning establishes the purchase quantities, typically derived from the projected demand, existing inventories, and other parameters such as minimum order quantity constraints. Purchasing is the day-to-day purchase order life-cycle management, ordering, receiving, and settlement of vendor invoices (also known as purchase to pay, or order to settlement cycle).

Logistics is typically transportation management and refers to consolidating orders and creating shipments for the inbound and outbound orders. It consists of load optimization, route optimization, carrier selection, tracking and tracing the shipments, and carrier freight management functions.

Warehousing processes add the capabilities for receiving, stocking, inventory management, cross-docking, staging, order fulfilment, packing, shipping, and inventory reconciliation at the warehouses.

The scope of supply chain functions primarily covers all aspects of inventory and distribution costs. Most aspects of supply chain are modelled using mathematical algorithms and standard packaged solutions allow these costs to be optimized without sacrificing the service levels. Hence the supply chain management directly plays to the bottom-line for a retailer. As retailers mature, the focus shifts from the revenues growth to cost-containment to manage profitable growth and optimizing the supply chain provides the key to manage it.

To successfully transition from a retail start-up to a stable, mature, and profitable business, retailers must grasp both, the merchandising and the supply chain functions. They must develop capabilities that would not only keep their products fresh and customers excited, but also run their operations smoothly and efficiently to survive and grow profitably.

Transportation has become quite popular in recent years. Automated transportation optimization solutions support the process in most large companies to create shipments for the inbound and outbound orders. What exactly happens in this optimization? Without going into the mathematical formulation and objective functions, here is a functional picture of what these solutions do.

Load Optimization: Load optimization creates the optimal loads for the standard trailer sizes. These could be optimized using the expected weight of the shipments or volume, depending on which one presents the loading constraint. The main objective of this part of optimization is simply to maximize the weight or volume capacity usage of the trailers for the shipments built.

The constraints while deciding on load optimization are generally the dates and routes the solution must find orders that can travel together in the same window of time to successfully create optimized loads.

Route Optimization: Route optimization selects the best route to minimize the cost of transportation. This could be a route where the shipments can travel on long-haul rates for the longest part of the route or where the route is a combination of multi-modal transportation options so that the longest leg of the shipments travels on rail. The constraints for this step can be existence of rate-contracts, availability of routes, and so on for the solution to select optimal routes.

Resource Optimization: Resource optimization finally selects the carrier and the equipment that the shipments will travel on. The objective here may be to minimize the cost or simply ensure reliable pick-up and delivery dates. Constraints that play into this step are availability of valid carrier contracts and capacities on selected routes.

While the steps here provide a functional understanding of the process, different vendor solutions may implement them differently or simultaneously. In fact, best solutions are those that have the ability to model all three cases simultaneously so that the output is globally optimized which simply means that instead of trying to create best loads first only to find that no available equipment can actually carry them on required dates, these solutions consider all constraints simultaneously to produce results that are feasible and optimized for the orders.

Chapter 16: Supply Chain and Merchandising

Retail is a complex industry to manage. Between the unpredictable seasons, finicky customers, and a volatile economy it presents a worthy challenge. Two foundational business capabilities in Merchandising and Supply Chain determine a Retailer's ability to compete. Merchandising gets the Customers, and Supply Chain gets the Products...

At the highest level, it is a simple concept. Buy, Distribute, and Sell. And as long as you can do that profitably, you are in business. That is where the rub is – profitably – an average departmental retail store can have tens of thousands of items to start with. Add to that the number of stores, formats, customer demographics, seasons, fashions, competitor across the road, weather, economy and you have a pretty hairy problem. The sheer number of independent variables that a retailer must contend with, in planning and executing is mind boggling.

However, understanding the two key processes in merchandising and supply chain can make or break a retailer. Building functional capabilities in these areas to flexibly address business needs can give a retailer competitive edge.

Get the Customer's Attention: Merchandising

Merchandising truly defines Retail. It is what makes a retailer unique, and provides the "niche". It provides the retailer its "identity". Wal-Mart shoppers know they will get lowest prices, but not necessarily the service, or variety. Upscale retailers like Harrods on the other hand are "identified" more with the chic image.

Merchandising has various sub-functions. It has a financial aspect and an assortment aspect.

Merchandise financial planning sets up a Retailer's plans, for revenues, inventory levels, mark-ups, gross margins, promotions, clearance etc. Planned targets for sales, and inventory are set in this process, so are the budgets for promotions, clearance, and marketing. These plans can be started at the top, and trickle down the organization, regional and product hierarchies. Some companies may also do a bottom up planning for this function and then reconcile the top-down numbers with the bottoms-up numbers.

Next the assortment plans are created. Assortment plans determine what will be sold where. Assortments may vary from store to store based on demographics, competition, weather, fashions, and new products. These plans typically start with the evaluation of the existing product and assortment portfolios, and establish the new assortments for the planning period. These assortment plans are then reconciled with the merchandising plans to make sure that the assortments can actually meet the financial budgets, and projections. These assortment plans are typically available at regional, store cluster, product class and sometimes at item levels.

Further down, the assortment plans then generate the macro and micro space planning. Macro space planning constrains the planning process based on logistics, distribution, and storage constraints in the supply chain. Micro space planning creates layouts that determine the product presentation in the stores, presentation quantities, and other displays.

Merchandise planning is primarily the top-line play for a retailer. This is the most important function in the growth stage for any retailer. Its importance does not diminish for mature retailers, though the strategy for mature companies normally shifts from top-line growth to bottom-line improvement; and therefore, cost control becomes more important than growing the top line. And that is where Supply Chain becomes important.

Get the Right Products at the Right Place at the Right Time: Supply Chain

Supply chain capabilities define the cost basis, and hence directly affect the competitiveness of a retailer. Supply chain efficiencies cut costs all around; inventories, transportation, warehousing. After the cost of merchandise, these (supply chain) costs are the biggest costs for a retailer. Even a small savings on these costs can mean millions of dollars directly going into the bottom line for most retailers. The good news is that unlike the cost of the merchandise, the supply chain costs are directly controllable by the retailer through better planning, optimization, and execution.

Supply chain typically covers the network planning, demand planning, supply planning, logistics, and distribution operations.

The stocking and selling locations together with the supply locations (vendor's shipping points) make the supply chain network. The supply chain network planning helps in optimally locating the distribution hubs, and supply points within a retailer's network of facilities. The network evaluation can result in facility relocations, and generally executed yearly, or sometimes less frequently.

Demand planning is the science of projecting future demand that must be replenished at each of the stocking, and selling locations. Sales history is required, and other inputs may allow modelling of seasonal demand, promotions, weather, and price changes. It produces a sales forecast, and accounts for inventory to determine the actual demand.

Supply planning typically covers sourcing, vendor management, inventory planning, replenishment planning, and purchase management. Sourcing establishes the process for finding and selecting vendors that the corporation will deal with. There may be supply contracts and relationship guidelines that are part of the process. Vendor management refers to on-going relationship management, and vendor performance evaluation. Inventory planning determines how much to stock to meet a desired service level, at selling locations, and at stocking locations.

Replenishment planning establishes the purchase quantities, typically derived from the projected demand, inventories, and ordering/stocking parameters such as minimum order constraints. Purchasing is the day-to-day purchase order life-cycle management, expediting, analysis, and settlement (also known as purchase to pay, or order to settlement cycle).

Next two areas of supply chain refer to the movement and stocking of goods along the supply lines. Logistics is typically transportation management, and refers to consolidating orders, load optimization, route optimization, carrier selection, tracking and tracing capabilities, and carrier freight management. Warehousing then adds the capabilities for receiving, stocking, pallet/case breaking; cross-docking, staging, packing, shipping, and inventory reconciliation.

The scope of supply chain functions primarily covers all aspects of costs related to inventory levels, stocking, and movement costs. Almost all aspects of supply chain can be modelled using mathematical algorithms, and standard packaged solutions allow these costs to be optimized without sacrificing the service levels. Hence the supply chain management directly plays to the bottom-line for a retailer. As retailers mature, the focus shifts from the revenues growth to cost-containment to continue profitable growth; and optimizing the supply chain provides the key to efficient operations.

Chapter 17: Retail's Silver Bullet

In the midst of a challenging economic environment and shifting consumer trends, retailers are taking even sharper look at the link between improved financial performance and managing end-to-end costs. As a result, the role of supply chain management (SCM) is in the middle of an era of renewed focus and innovation.

Until now the primary strategic approach for retail growth had been to "add new stores." Additionally, some processes such as merchandising and ordering were carried out at a decentralized store level. Now with retailers facing a different economic landscape, there is no market for larger upfront investments. In preparation for future growth and in order to bridge financially to better times, retailers are reining in costs and centralizing their operations to improve efficiency and reduce expenditures.

Faced with slowing revenues, leading retailers have identified supply chain management as an area where costs can be controlled and further reduced. They are placing a greater corporate focus on the strategic opportunities within SCM and taking a comprehensive look at how they can increase efficiency, decrease costs and improve customer satisfaction.

The Retail Industry Leaders Association (RILA) represents the world's largest and most innovative retail companies. RILA members have revolutionized the supply chain management and goods movement.

Although SCM has long played a critical role in retail, the challenges of a global economic recession and ever-tightening budgets are driving leading retailers to rely more heavily on supply chain as a solution for overall organizational success.

Revenues are stagnant in many retail organizations, costs are viewed as controllable. In particular, the expenses falling under the control of SCM executives are receiving strong attention from the top of the organization. SCM executives now find themselves in the spotlight and must perform their brand of magic to save the show.

Additionally, to offset declined consumer spending, supply chain management executives are focusing their efforts on reducing excess inventory.

To be effective, SCM executives need to closely manage the total cost of global procurement, streamline inventories, and decrease transportation expenses, while ensuring product availability and strong customer service.

The tools that enable superior supply chain management and generate a competitive advantage separate the best-in class retailer from the laggard retailer. Four major tools used by leading players within retail supply chain management are.
1. Leverage strong distribution networks that are capable of supporting high volumes.

2. Create flexible capacity to adjust supply chain infrastructure and support unanticipated fluctuation in demand.
3. Align inside and outside the organization to break down silos and manage processes more holistically.
4. Continually develop the internal talent pool to enhance the quality of the workforce.

These best-in-class capabilities are key to the future success of retail supply chain management and central to the vitality and fortitude of retailers.

Ultimately, the retailers who are best able to respond to changes in consumer demand while driving down costs will come out ahead. Not only will they provide more value to their organization in the short term, but they also will put themselves in an ideal position to thrive when the marketplace recovers and consumer trends improve.

Chapter 18: Controlling Cost of Sales through Supply Chain Competencies

Supply chain competence affects your bottom-line in more direct ways than you might realize. In this chapter we will review the role of controlling cost of sales through supply chain competencies and its effect on the corporate financial statements.

The cost of sales appears on the income statement right below the revenues. The difference between the revenues and the cost of sales is the gross profit. Therefore, the cost of sales directly determines the gross profit of a firm and that is directly responsible for the firm's bottom-line. It has several aliases; it may be called cost of goods sold, cost of products, cost of products sold or something else similar in connotation. That is not important. What is important is what constitutes the cost of sales.

Typically, for manufacturers and retailers, it is also the second biggest number on the income statement after the revenues. In fact, for the financial year 2009, the COGS was 50% of 2009 revenues for P&G, 76% of the total revenues for Wal-Mart, and 70% of sales at Target for FY2009. Therefore, if one had to start looking at reducing costs, COGS fits the bill nicely. This is the largest pie of expense in an organization and even a small reduction in this will naturally generate a large impact on the firm's bottom-line.

What does cost of sales consist of?

Cost of sales generally includes all direct expenses related to the products or services that a firm sells. For manufacturers, this typically includes the cost of raw materials and purchased sub-assemblies, cost of conversion to the finished goods like the direct labour used to run a plant, depreciation of the plant and machinery, or things like the coolant oil needed to cut metal on the turning centres, cost of freight to transport raw-materials to its factories, warehousing costs to maintain the finished-goods stocks and shipping costs to ship them to their customers. In a retail scenario, the cost of sales will include the cost of merchandise and the cost of freight from its suppliers to its warehouses, and the cost of distribution from its warehouses to its stores. In summary it includes all direct expenses related to the value-adding activities of the firm in the cost of sales.

So how can supply chain competency affect the cost of sales?

Almost all expenses related to the value-adding activities are controlled through the supply chain processes and the efficacy of these processes determines the cost basis of the activity. Take the warehousing costs, for example, automating the warehouse planning and execution activities through a warehouse management and execution system can increase the number of cases handled on inbound and outbound shipments for every labour-hour employed. The freight costs can be reduced by employing a better process for planning shipments that can reduce the miles driven, enhance the equipment utilization rates, or consolidate shipments to reduce freight. Any way you look at it, developing supply chain process competencies affects the process efficiencies that in turn, affect the cost of sales and hence your profitability.

Following are some of most common expenses included in the COGS and the supply chain process that can potentially optimize it.

1. Cost Component of COGS
2. Supply Chain Process Managing the Cost Component
3. Financial Metrics Affected
4. Direct Materials and Supplies, Cost of Raw Materials and Inputs (for manufacturers), or Merchandise (for retailers), etc.
5. Forecasting, Replenishment, Inventory Management (raw materials), Sourcing, Purchasing
6. Gross Margin, EBITDA, Inventory, Inventory Turnover, Current Assets, Working Capital, Return on Assets.
7. Direct Labour, Cost of Transformation (production, manufacturing, processing, etc.), Depreciation, Direct Manufacturing Overheads, etc.
8. Production Planning, Factory Planning, Resource Planning, Inventory (work-in-progress) Management
9. Gross Margin, EBITDA, Working Capital, Return on Capital Employed.

10. Cost of Freight (all inbound, outbound, and intra-facility transfers of material)
11. Transportation Management
12. Gross Margin, EBITDA, Working Capital.
13. Cost of Warehousing, Inventory Shrink, Obsolescence, Mark-downs, Handling, Inventory Carrying
14. Warehouse Management, Labour Management, Inventory Management (finished goods or merchandise)
15. Gross Margin, EBITDA, Working Capital.

The cost of materials, whether raw materials or merchandise, can be reduced through strategic sourcing, bid optimization, and supplier contracts-based optimization. Good demand and supply management practices also help in reducing the cost of materials by reducing obsolescence. Obsolete inventory typically results in merchandise clearance and write-offs both of which increase the total costs of materials.

Distribution costs primarily consist of warehousing and transportation. Supply chain processes that can help reduce these costs are network planning, warehouse management, and transportation management.

The warehousing management capabilities reduce the warehousing costs through better use of space, better inventory management in the warehouse, automation, and optimized labour scheduling.

Network planning can reduce the cost of distribution through optimal positioning of the distribution centres with respect to the suppliers and stores.

Transportation management capabilities help reduce the distribution costs by optimizing shipments that reduce the total miles driven and enhance the container and trailer volume utilization. Better fleet management capabilities can increase the efficiency of the fleet and freight invoice automation can reduce the expenses related to validating and paying for freight.

Manufacturing costs can be reduced through better scheduling and factory planning processes. Supply chain optimization solutions that allow modelling of the demand, available inventory, available resources, operations, and sequencing constraints are typically used to produce feasible manufacturing schedules that can optimize the usage of assets and resources to produce manufacturing schedules that drive most profitable product-mix for the given demand or maximize the demand fulfilment for given orders. Increasing the asset utilization reduces need for investing in capital assets thus reducing long-term debt used to finance capital investments. In turn, it positively impacts return on capital employed by reducing the total current liabilities.

Major labour costs for the retailers occur in the warehouses and the stores, and for manufacturers, they are in the factories. Warehouse management processes can help directly reduce the labour costs in the warehouses, by better labour planning, scheduling,

93

and task tracking. Better demand forecasting in the stores helps in streamlining the labour plans in the stores. Manufacturing labour costs are minimized through better scheduling and factory planning capabilities that can model the material and asset constraints to produce feasible labour plans.

Any reduction in the cost of sales directly translates into increased margins assuming the other factors remain constant.

Chapter 19: Supply Chain Analytics and Data Discovery

When planning supply chain analytics, plan for conventional warehouse based reporting and analytics; and more sophisticated data exploration environment for data mining and statistical analysis. While the conventional reporting and analysis helps track and report on the efficiency of the supply chain processes, the data exploration tools can actually enhance your ability to continuously optimize the process parameters to function at their best. The good news is that you can use the same data warehouse for both the purposes.

Let us expand on the two underlying concepts for clarity

1. Reporting and Analytics

This is the more conventional, familiar and easier to understand area of analysis. Most companies have reporting environments that allow them to generate standard reports. Some also have analytical environments that allow users to interactively generate multi-dimensional views for dissecting the data as they need. Most such environments are based on data warehouses that pull planning and transaction data from the supply chain applications, and present this data with common master data references. Some well known characteristics of such environments are as under.

a. **Pre-defined data models and dimensions:** Data models are pre-defined and rigid. The dimensions are constructed based on the original data model design and any changes need IT effort. The metrics are generally a combination of pre-defined standard metrics, as well as user created ad-hoc metrics that are based on formulas and use the existing data in the warehouse.

b. **Processed and harmonized data:** The contextual data such as items, locations, time, vendors, customers, etc. (also known as master data) is pre-processed and harmonized across all reporting applications. This is important because very few corporations currently have enterprise master data management systems. Any enterprise level reporting needs consistent master data to pull together the information from various applications and geographies and present an enterprise view.

c. **Tactical or strategic, but repetitive and consistent metrics:** This is the defining attribute of these systems. The metrics are consistent and repetitive. It is this characteristic that makes the warehouse's rigidly defined data models possible.

d. **Ad-hoc analysis components do not equate to data discovery:** While ad-hoc reporting may be available, it is limited to providing user driven metrics that are computed on-demand. The analytics may provide multiple data views by user selected dimensions, and even consolidate data/metrics as user selects a different view. However none of this provides a true data discovery function that we would talk about in the following section on data exploration.

The conventional reporting and analytics provides a great way to build and report metrics on several supply chain areas, such as inventory, supplier compliance and sales analysis.

2. Data Exploration and Discovery

A lot of supply chain applications leverage data patterns. As these data patterns change and emerge, these applications provide solutions that are less than optimal. To keep these solutions at their most optimal levels, a data exploration and discovery environment should be created along-side the supply chain data warehouse. Such capability can provide clues to power users when the underlying data patterns change and allow them to change application configurations pro-actively rather than react to such changes using a conventional reporting environment.

A data exploration/discovery environment has the following characteristics.
    a. No pre-defied data models, or dimensions: The data discovery models typically have no pre-defined models. They thrive on raw data. The models for discovery are created by the power users with a specific problem in mind.

These models could be retained for future simulations, or thrown away after the target problem has been resolved, or the underlying reasons have been discovered.

b. As an example, consider a product profitability profiling model using data mining techniques. Once defined using the historical data on profitability, this model can be reused to "predict" the profitability profile of new merchandise before introducing the new products.

c. On the other hand an inventory profiling model may change from one season to another as the underlying parameters that drive such profiles change with time.

d. Involves data discovery: These models use raw data and discovery algorithms to find new and hidden patterns in data. The user does not have to "know" the data before using it, rather the system "discovers" the relationships, similarities, profiles, etc, that exist in the data and provides the output of such "discovery" to the user for review and decision support.

e. For example if you wish to create a profile of poorly performing stores, the user does not need to know what parameters to look for. Rather the discovery algorithms can group the poorly performing stores by exploring the historical data, and "discover" the parameters that are most relevant for such profiling.

f. Uses raw data: Unlike the reporting environments, the data discovery algorithms need raw, unprocessed data to be most effective.

g. Helps in setting up decision parameters for downstream processes: The data discovery and exploration tools are decision support applications that help the power users analyze data and make decisions on how best to run other related processes. For example demand forecasting, seasonal planning, strategic sourcing processes can all benefit from such analysis by detecting changes in data patterns through discovery.

Relatively long term and strategic in nature

There are more supply chain processes that can benefit from data exploration and discovery. Some of these are flow path optimization, store cluster optimization for determining merchandise assortments, and targeted marketing etc. In fact any process that can benefit from the following functions is a good example of where data exploration and discovery can be leveraged.

a. Processes that depend on statistical analysis such as inventory planning, demand planning, and supply planning.

b. Processes that can leverage data mining and clustering techniques such as creating inventory groups for maintaining inventory policies, store groups for assortments, merchandise groups for profitability.

c. Processes that can leverage simulation such as inventory planning, allocations, etc.

While most corporations plan and invest large amounts of capital on the conventional reporting solutions, the high-end data exploration and discovery solutions are comparatively rare. Part of the reason is lack of understanding on how these tools can be used as well as lack of people skilled in such tools who also understand the business of supply chain.

Most of the techniques mentioned above in the context of data discovery and exploration are part of a larger discipline known as predictive modelling and analysis. The predictive modelling techniques are used for projecting and managing risks and are quite well adapted in the financial and insurance industries. However their use for modelling and managing supply chains is still emerging.

Chapter 20: Spend Analysis for Retailers

A little line under the Revenues in the Income Statement of the companies shows COGS, or Cost of Goods Sold. If you are a retailer, this line captures your biggest business expense. For most retailers COGS can add up to 60-65% of their revenues, and largely represents the cost of merchandise purchased over the year.

Spend Analysis for direct (merchandise) purchases helps retailers track and analyze this (largest) expense as well as provides them with a great tool for managing their purchasing decisions. With a little innovation, spend analysis can also help the retailers manage their cash-flows, provide negotiating leverage with the vendors, maintain contract compliance, and keep a close tab at the cost trends.

Total Spend Analysis for Retailers

Total Spend Analysis brings together various important facts related to the direct merchandise spend. It can contain the actual spend, planned/budgeted spend, committed spend, and can also provide projected spend through projected accruals and forecasts. Most of these numbers are simple to calculate and provide a wealth of information into one of the largest COGS items. The total spend is often organized by vendor, item, organization/location and merchandise category.

These dimensions (vendor, item, organization/location and merchandise category) can have company specific hierarchies so that the data can be rolled up, or dis-aggregated along the hierarchy levels as required.

Actual Spend is simply the value of all order line items that have been "closed" and settled. This can be easily calculated with the PO data available from the PO management systems (or ERPs). This number exists only for current and historical time buckets.

Planned Spend (or purchasing budget) is generally sourced from the merchandise financial planning systems. Merchandise Financial Planning (MFP) is a top-down exercise that provides planned spend targets generally required to support the financial plan of the company for revenues, profitability, and inventory. Some MFP solutions also allow a bottom-up approach for setting up these targets, that are then reconciled with the top-down numbers before publishing the final plan numbers. This number exists for historical and future time buckets.

Projected Committed Spend is the cumulative cost of all open purchases that are committed to vendors through confirmed purchase orders. This is also a simple calculation that adds up the price on all PO line items that are "open", and not yet "received" (and therefore not yet accrued). This data is normally sourced from the PO management systems (or ERPs). This number is meaningful only for current and future time buckets.

Projected Accruals are calculated using vendor acknowledgments, ASN (advanced shipping notices), or simply the need dates on the open purchase orders. This is the spend that is expected to accrue based on projected delivery of inventory from the vendors. If required, a longer term projection for the cash outflow can also be made using statistical projection using the historic data. These numbers are meaningful only for current and future time buckets.

Projected Available Spend (or Open to Buy) dollars/pounds can then be calculated as the cumulative actual spend till the current time bucket versus the planned (budgeted) dollars/pounds for the whole planning horizon or season. These numbers are most commonly used for seasonal products to track and control the seasonal item spend during mid-season. However, the concept is equally applicable for any item with a generic definition of planning horizon.

If there are supplier contracts that either have purchase obligations, tier pricing, volume discounts, cash-back rebates, etc., then it also makes sense to bring in the contractual data into such analysis. This is a cumulative value of all purchases made under a specific contract, as well as the contract volume/tier threshold information at which cost changes, or discounts/rebates become available.

Depending on the role, different will use this data for different reasons. However spend analysis provides a powerful decision support system for all users that manage the purchasing activity in an organization.

103

Buyers who are responsible for certain vendors may be interested in spend reports by month by vendor across all vendor-items and locations. If the contract data is available, buyers can compare actual, accrued and committed spend with the contractual obligations to determine compliance, as well as current rebates, discounts and pricing tiers. Buyers can typically use this information to track the total spend; for vendor negotiation; contract compliance; and to avail proper contract pricing/rebates/discounts. When the analysis tool allows projections of the spend into the future (using historical data), it can provide valuable demand information for negotiating future contracts with the vendors, for evaluating bids, and awarding the contracts to maximize the cost-savings.

Merchants may want to see the same spend data by categories managed by them; with the intention of controlling and manipulating the seasonal spend. They can also use the data to determine profitability trends at the merchandise category, vendor or regions. (YOY) Year over year comparison for spend, when combined with the revenues for the same product category provide a clear picture of profitability trends for the merchandise categories. Similarly, spend trending is another useful analysis tool. Trending quickly shows if the costs are going up, down or stabilizing. When the revenue trends are mixed with the cost trends, it provides an easy way to create a powerful visual picture of the profitability by category, regions, or a vendor.

Finance Analysts also need this spend data organized by regions with the intention of managing invoices, accruals, settlements, and the cash flow. This analysis can be used for projecting and managing the future accruals and outbound cash flow.

Spend analysis is one of the easier analytics applications to build and use. It primarily requires purchase data that is easily obtained from most ERP, or legacy systems; and can be quickly enriched with other data from financial planning and settlement (AP) systems. The analysis is easy to understand, and directly affects the largest single spends for retailers.

Chapter 21: A Framework for Measuring Supply Chain Costs

In my opinion, there are two main long term trends in the environment that will impact supply chain strategies one is the costs and redistribution of costs/incomes; and second is environmental consciousness.

Let us explore what constitutes the supply chain costs and the specific processes that impact these costs. Some of the supply chain costs are crisply defined, readily available, and widely used in the industry. Others are less well known, and tend to get lost in the heaps of corporate data. However evaluating supply chain costs requires that we understand them, invest in defining them as clearly as possible, have processes to capture, report, and analyze them. Only such a complete picture of supply chain costs can truly drive new initiatives, find gaps in existing processes, and help in continually improving the cost and efficiency of the supply chain operations.

To clearly understand the impact of supply chain costs, corporations need to develop a "cost framework" to define, develop, and measure these costs. The discussions below helps in understanding what such a framework should look like, the scope of such costs, and how they affect the total supply chain costs for an enterprise.

To understand the scope of these costs, we will organize them into three categories

Direct Costs

These are the direct costs of merchandise, and services. These are easy to capture, understand, and report. Examples of these costs are the cost of merchandise (purchase orders), cost of freight (load tenders), cost of warehousing services (warehousing costs), and so on. As most of these costs are captured through standard enterprise transactions like purchase orders, or load tenders, they are easy to capture and measure at the corporate level. The complexity arises when there is a requirement to allocate these costs across organizational entities such as product groups, or regions, etc. Such cost allocation is not unusual, and helps in establishing profitability of separate business groups, merchandise portfolios and so on. Though a well thought out accounting structure should be able to support such allocations objectively.

Spend Analysis directly focuses on this aspect of the supply chain costs. Consolidating all direct spend costs across the enterprise, helps in understanding the total spend layout with the vendors and service providers, and allow the enterprises to negotiate better deals and volume discounts.

   a. Consolidate all spend by merchandise category, vendor, and service providers. Look for volume discounts, and negotiate on other costs such as credit terms, returns, quality, etc.

   b. Analyze the merchandise demand; establish long term contracts for merchandise with stable and predictable demand. Implement software systems for bid evaluation and purchase planning when multiple suppliers are viable.

c. Evaluate possibility of using traditional and reverse auctions for one time and/or seasonal purchases where product attributes allow for such purchasing strategies.

d. Implement transportation optimization systems to directly impact the freight costs from the cost equation.

e. Evaluate all service provider contracts with transaction based fee and analyze historical usage for possible reductions by converting these transaction-fee contracts to fixed-fee contracts.

Process Costs

Process costs relate to the organizational teams that directly support supply chain processes. These processes may provide critical supply chain decisions to support operations, and support compliance requirements for regulatory purposes. Examples of such processes are demand management (forecasting, inventory planning, and replenishment teams), supply management (purchasing, expediting teams), logistics (shipment planners, load and route planners, and dispatchers), and global trade teams supporting imports and exports. These are direct personnel costs and can be impacted positively by improving process efficiency that leads to smaller teams handling the same volume of transactions. Such efficiency improvements can be a result of process automation, processes simplification, or process elimination.

Evaluate if the process can be automated through a system, completely or partly. Most IT applications provide automation for the transaction processing; some do so for the planning processes as well. Supply chain planning solutions routinely provide optimization based algorithms that can provide decision support for complex situations, such as determining optimal inventory levels at various locations. Such systems make processes efficient, as well as more effective by handling large amounts of data and computations that are otherwise impossible to be processed manually. They also allow more frequent reviews of supply chain policy parameters (such as inventory levels, flow-paths, seasonal inventory management, forecasting parameters, etc.) to keep them aligned with the changing demand and supply scenarios.

Evaluate if the process steps can be simplified, or eliminated. For example, consider whether all purchase orders need managerial approvals, or is there is a possibility that purchases within defined constraints (purchase value, vendor status, resulting inventory level etc.) can be made without such approval. Evaluate processes where all transactions are currently reviewed manually, and consider defining transaction profiles so that the system can identify exceptions for manual review while automatically processing the rest. Replenishment planning, purchasing, load tenders are all examples of processes where exception based management can be effectively implemented and manual effort can be reduced.

Technology Costs

The last category of supply chain costs are technology costs. Some examples of these costs include the software and hardware costs of deploying supply chain systems at the corporate office, dimensioning system and RF handheld units at the warehouse, and the geo-location tracking units on the trucks. The technology enables faster processing time for planning, near real-time execution, continuous visibility of inventory and operations from end-to-end, and enables decision support systems that leverage complex mathematical models to provide optimal results. But all the technology adds its own cost to the supply chain. As technology continues to play ever bigger part in supply chains, managing technology costs becomes more important. This is a difficult area as it straddles the business and IT groups, and requires that both collaborate closely to measure, contain, and evolve a technology strategy that allows for a cost-aware technology evolution with flexible supply chain solutions. This is easier said than done, however, these costs must be measured before they can be contained.

1. Establish an existing and to-be technology roadmap for supply chain. Create a checklist of business best practices and establish the gaps in current technology, prioritize new technology, and plan a purposeful adoption rather than an ad-hoc reactive evolution.

2. Establish costs of all technical resources, software, hardware and people. Establish maintenance and projected upgrade expenses.

111

Clearly identify what the technology costs, and what it provides in return.

3. Evaluate technology diversity; while diversity in general is good, it may not be so in technology. Too many technologies quickly become expensive to maintain due to specialized skill requirements, hardware requirements, and annual maintenance fees. Consolidate common standards for technology stacks across applications, adopt SOA architecture for custom developed applications, evaluate annual license renewals for continued need, consolidate hardware vendors, virtualize, have consistent application and technology architecture, have business readiness plans in place through backups and disaster recovery. Empower enterprise architecture.

Measure, question, evaluate, and evolve!

Most corporations do not have a consolidated view of costs of their supply chains. This constraints their ability to accurately identify opportunities and problem areas, prioritize supply chain investments, and constrains their ability to execute simple profitability analysis accurately. Creating a broad cost view of the supply chain requires careful analysis, planning, and processes to gather data, however, it allows for quickly analyzing the impact of changes, even predict such changes, and manage an ever-evolving supply chain for the optimal corporate efficiency.

Chapter 22: Financial Metrics and the Chief Finance Officer

You think your CFO (Chief Finance Officer) controls your company's financial performance, think again.

Corporations are economic entities. Most commercial corporations exist with a single motive; to productively engage in economic activity and create wealth for their investors, and value for their customers, and employees. The financial metrics measure the success of these corporations. Conventionally the office of the CFO owns these metrics, and takes responsibility for maintaining healthy financial numbers.

Take a deeper look and you will find that there are few of these numbers that the office of the CFO directly controls. And that is where you, me and everyone else comes in; while the CFOs own and report these numbers, it is really everyone who affects them and therefore directly controls them.

Conventionally, BI (Business Intelligence) has looked at metrics as Strategic, Tactical, and Operational. While this view provides a good classification it really is no good from the point of view of answering – "so what"?

Here is an innovative layering of the financial metrics that will help you go in the right direction by providing discrete actionable information.

Indicator (Windsock) Metrics

The top layer is what I call the Indicator Metrics. These are the top level metrics that provide a quick overview of company's financial health. They are composite in nature and are made up of other metrics. One key example from this layer is ROA (Return on Assets). ROA primarily measures the effectiveness with which a corporation uses its assets in generating the profits. Metrics similar to ROA in intent are Return on Equity, and Return on Capital, and Margins (gross, net, pre-tax, operating or any other kind of Margins).

Let us look at the ROA. It is typically a product of Margin and Asset Turnover. Margin is simply profit on sales, and directly measures the profitability of the business. Asset Turnover measures how many times the assets are used over to generate the sales; therefore measuring how effectively a corporation uses its assets.

If ROA is a concern comparing with industry averages you can tell whether asset utilization is an issue or profitability. In mature, competitive markets, profitability is less controllable due to external market factors that are hard to predict and control, but asset turnover efficiency can provide a corporation competitive edge.

These metrics generally tell the direction in which a corporation should look for efficiencies, hence the name Indicator Metrics, or Windsock Metrics. There are quite a few other metrics in this layer such as the various Ratios/Liquidity metrics, and some activity and leverage metrics.

Dashboard (Traffic Light) Metrics

The second layer of metrics is also composite in nature. These metrics form the basis of the top level indicator metrics. However these metrics provide a good indicator of the operations that need review. Continuing from the ROA definition above, we had established Margin as one of the factors (that contributes towards ROA). Margin consists of profit over sales. The profit in this equation is generally NOPAT (net operating profit after taxes). Now NOPAT itself consists of Sales, COGS, SG&A, and Taxes. With the exception of Taxes (taxes also can be managed to an extent), others are directly controllable. Again comparisons to industry averages can quickly establish which of these (say between COGS, and SG&A "Selling, General and Administrative Expenses") have the most potential for improvement.

Major components for COGS for a retail company will be merchandise (purchase) costs, distribution (supply chain) costs, labour (store and warehouse) costs, and other indirect costs (for example the advertising). All these numbers need to be controlled and watched closely to align to the projected/desired COGS target.

I call the metrics in this layer as the traffic light metrics as these metrics can be computed on a more frequent basis, and colour coded (like a Dashboard)

115

to be Red/Yellow/Green to drive the prevalent action bias in a corporation.

Actionable (Tuning Knob) Metrics

Finally the last layer of metrics that touches directly upon the daily operations of the corporation, and therefore provides the "Tuning" ability to affect the higher levels above. Drilling down from our example above, cost of Merchandise is a large component in the COGS for retailers. This cost itself is direct cost of the merchandise, as well as the cost of generating POs, and managing their life-cycles, cost of handling customer returns, cost of wrong shipments (inbound and out), cost of bad quality, cost of measuring process efficiencies (supplier compliance, conformance), cost of settlement, etc. These are distinct costs that arise from distinct business processes. And hence they measure the efficiency (or inefficiency) of these processes, giving the culprits or potential processes to be improved.

These metrics provide the tuning knobs that affect the dash-board and indicator metrics; because these metrics directly point to a business processes that need improvement. For example, if the cost of managing purchase orders is high (compared to industry standards), then the process of creating and managing POs needs to be investigated. The higher costs may exist because of an inefficient PO management process/system, or (surprisingly) reveal a sound PO management; but an inefficient replenishment system that creates an unnecessarily high number of POs. Either way; these metrics

116

provide a directly actionable result and therefore can help in tuning the higher level metrics that are more indicative in nature.

Operational (day-in-life) Metrics

These metrics help a corporation run their daily business more effectively, like a list of orders to be expedited, or fulfilled. They may not directly point to the weaker processes but provide information for root cause analysis.

So Who Controls the Financials Then?

With the above context, think again about who really controls the financial performance of your company? The metrics that actually allow you to impact the financial performance are contained in business processes that a corporation adopts. These business processes range from everything in supply chain to merchandising to manufacturing planning and store operations. And none of these functions are planned, strategized, organized, or executed by the CFO's office. Next time you see a poorly performing number try and dig deeper, you will find what you can do about it by looking at the underlying process(es) and have an impact on your company's financials. Then of course a progressive CFO's office can help too by actually supporting such analysis! Pray you have one!

Chapter 23: Multi-channel Retailer's Supply Chain Management.

Almost all big retailers today will consider themselves as a multi-channel retail company. Web-commerce has taken a strong hold on the retail landscape, and emerging user habits continue to point to an ever increasing share of retail spends on the web.

Retail is one of the largest sectors in the US economy. The U.S. Bureau of Economic Analysis reported the 2007 GDP of the country to be $14,000 billion, out of which $4,041 billion was retail. That makes retail account for almost a third of the total economic activity in the nation. Within retail, the CAGR for conventional retail is approximately 4.8%, while the online retail sector has grown at a CAGR of 25.4%. While the online growth must plateau out with time, it is still reported to be anywhere between 11 to 17%, with Forrester Research estimating the online retail to cross $200 billion this year. The point is; online retail is here to stay; most retailers have invested heavily in the technology to support online retail channels; and will continue to do so as this is the most logical growth channel at present time.

Having the ability to sell through multiple channels is simply the start. Multi-channel retailing offers so many potential opportunities for the traditional retailer to create synergy, enhance operational efficiencies, reduce costs, and enhance user experience that it is an obvious choice to implement

119

these changes that would allow a retailer to achieve most of the above.

On-line retailers have given tough competition to traditional retailing; however, traditional retailers have a lot more going for them if they choose to leverage their assets when planning a multi-channel play. The three main areas to consider are as follows.

Integrated Assortment Planning

1. Do you have integrated assortment planning capabilities for physical and virtual channels?
2. That supports consolidated assortment planning, and therefore supports corporate level merchandise planning objectives.
3. That supports compatible assortment spread, with core assortment defining the core category attributes, and extended assortment supporting the cores assortment and extending these category attributes.
4. That allows for integrated product and category portfolio analysis for profitability, affinity, market basket, and similar analysis.
5. That allows for aligning all the channels with the customer segmentation, and product positioning approach supporting corporate strategy and goals.
6. Do you have clearly identified core and extended assortments?
7. Core assortment that is common to physical stores, and the virtual channels. The core assortment is targeted at the core customers of the retailer, and depending on the retailer's

product positioning; this may be generic, or highly differentiated.

8. Extended assortment expands the core assortment, and is typically only available through non-store channels. This further accentuates the targeted segmentation and positioning of the retailer.

9. Core assortment is best suited for leveraging common logistics planning, execution, and operations. This is typically not a candidate for vendor drop-ship operations.

10. Extended assortment should be evaluated for fulfilment options that may be fully owned, or operated by the retailer. Such options include vendor drop-ship where the volumes are low, and/or product differentiation is high; VMI (vendor managed inventory), 3PL fulfilment options, etc.

11. Clearance and price realization.

12. Having a common assortment also supports pricing strategies for best price realization, seasonal ramp-up and downs, regional changes in demand across channels, and categories.

Integrated Supply Planning

1. Do you have the capabilities for consolidated demand and supply planning?

2. That allows to plan for all the merchandise demand together irrespective of the channel that would finally sell it?

3. That allows you to have a consolidated view of all forecasted demand, on-hand, and on-order inventories?
4. That allows you to have an enterprise-wide view of inventory layers?
5. Do your processes support consolidating sourcing, negotiating, and ordering?
6. That allows you to leverage total demand across channels, and therefore allow you to have a clear view of the total projected spend with a vendor for all categories of merchandise?
7. That helps you negotiating the right contracts, at the right prices, and optimizes the contract terms?
8. That help you raise and manage common purchase orders for the common merchandise, across all the channels; while simultaneously allowing you to allocate dynamically as the vendor acknowledgements, ASN, and merchandise arrives?
9. That helps you construct and leverage a consolidated projected inventory view?
10. Do you have common warehousing, and distribution operations?
11. That allows you to leverage the same inventory stock for replenishing stores, as well as for fulfilling online demand?
12. That allows you to provide in-store pick-ups for core as well as extended merchandise?
13. That allows you to leverage your dedicated fleet to make multi-stop multi-leg deliveries on their daily routes combining store, and customer deliveries when such opportunities

exist? How about picking up customer returns?

14. Do you leverage consolidated inbound shipments planning?
15. To reduce the total inbound shipment expense on transportation?

Integrated Store Operations

1. Do you have the capabilities for supporting a unified customer experience across all your channels, call, click, mail, or visit?
2. That supports a common customer view?
3. That supports a common order, and fulfilment view?
4. That supports a common pricing, will-call, delivery options?
5. That supports a seamless "customer case management" for enhanced customer satisfaction?
6. That supports a common product catalogue that is dynamically configurable for supporting a call centre customer service rep, a web store front, or a store kiosk?
7. Can your systems support endless aisles?
8. By having a common catalogue across channels, physical stores, and web-stores?
9. By having a consolidated near real-time view of all inventories across all channels and stores; and the ability to view, reserve, and open inventories across these entities?
10. By having all the capabilities available to all associates supporting customers irrespective

of their location, channel, and store affiliations?
11. Can you leverage all the channels, and fulfilment options for product clearance and final disposition events to optimize your realized average prices?
12. By dynamically moving inventories where desirable?
13. Or by deploying multiple fulfilment methods and selling channels that support direct delivery to customer, or store pick-ups?

Here are some of the signs of our times

1. Recession, we knew it all along except that now it is official!
2. Deflation, the stories are everywhere even though they don't add up, though let us assume some deflationary pressures may actually exist and continue for some time.
3. Credit crunch, less said the better. This is probably the root cause of major financial failures for many a companies. Central all over the world are throwing reams of money at the problem but it is still out there threatening businesses, large and small that need debt for short term and long term obligations.

What does this mean to retailers?

Pretty much the same thing, as all of the above conditions result into low demand for goods and services, pressure on pricing power, and tight credit for consumers as well as retailers.

This adds up to the following net results.

1. Top line impact. Low top line growth as consumers cut their spending due to recessionary pressures, job losses, uncertain financial conditions and tight consumer credit. All of these will result into low to no top line growth, and in some cases it may very well shrink.

2. Bottom line impact. Low profitability, fuelled by increased competition, too little demand, too little disposable income that all adds up to pressure on cutting prices further to retain the sales, and hurts the bottom line.

3. Cost of goods sold "COGS" impact. Higher cost of operations, driven by the tight credit and higher cost of money when it is available. Add to that the volatility of demand, and the desire to maintain good inventory levels to service customers when they do step in and buy.

So what should a retailer to do?

There really are not many options. In good times, you could follow a top line growth strategy effectively, but when the sales tank due to depressed consumer demand, there is only one strategy that works: laser sharp focus on the Cost and Efficiency. For the financially inclined, cost of goods sold "COGS" and Asset Turnover.

A good supply chain strategy can deliver on both of these fronts.

In fact, supply chains are all about costs and efficiency. Anything you do better in your supply chain management is bound to affect either of the two. Take for example, inventory planning processes. If enhancements to this process results in lower inventory, your inventory turnover goes up affecting the Asset Turnover positively. Assuming that the process improvements result in better fulfilment but do not affect inventory levels, the cost of operations for fulfilment and cost of lost sales goes down through better inventory deployment. Either way you come out ahead. Take transportation optimization, you reduce the miles, and have a direct impact on cost of transportation and hence cost of goods sold "COGS". Take forecasting improvements to have higher accuracy, and once again you save the cost of lost sales through better planning and deployment of inventories.

In fact any supply chain process improvement whether it is in planning or execution, network design or supply planning, demand planning or warehousing; all lead to either direct cost savings affecting the cost of goods sold "COGS", or more efficient use of assets affecting the Asset Turnover.

The next question of course is which is more important? Cost or Efficiency? Well that really depends!

It depends on what does the retailer want to achieve? If the retailer has good operating cash flow (and hence no need to borrow funds from the market), your efforts should be more focused on direct cost savings that will translate into the bottom line gains. If operating cash flow is an issue; and, it is if your survival depends on it, then profitability is a secondary consideration, and efficient use of resources may make more sense specially in a market where credit is either not available or the cost of servicing credit is simply unacceptable.

Rather than closing all initiatives, corporations should analyze and understand the impact of each current supply chain initiative. Then they should re-prioritize using the analysis, and their current needs. For reprioritization, follow the steps below.

1. List all your current supply chain initiatives. Note where in their deployment life-cycle these initiatives are, what are the sunk costs, and what are the estimated costs to finish them?
2. Classify these initiatives into those affecting Costs, and those affecting Efficiency.
3. For those affecting costs, determine the impact on cost of goods sold "COGS"; for those impacting efficiency, determine the impact on Asset Turnover.
4. Establish the immediate organizational priority between Costs and Efficiency.
5. Re-prioritize the current initiatives based on the above information.

Chapter 24: Distribution Options for Retailers

When it comes to distribution, Retailers have many options. These are Direct to Store, conventional Warehouse based "stock and distribute", or Cross-dock (or flow-through) models. Each of these options affects the supply chain efficiencies and costs.

Distribution Models for Retail

Understanding the costs and having processes to measure these costs provides an objective way to evaluate the impact of selecting these options. Most real-life situations will be complex enough to demand simultaneous deployment of all the three options for differing set of products and locations. But the cost analysis still helps to know what these sets should ideally be.

Cost Elements Relevant to Distribution

Some of these costs are harder to measure than others, but almost all of them can be objectively estimated for a good comparison among the available options for the selected set of products.

While the cost elements provide good data points for decision making, there is more to be considered.

We will look at the impact of these options on the twin supply chain parameters of lead-time and inventory. It is important to understand the interaction of costs with these two core parameters. For example, a shorter lead-time to replenish the store demand helps in better fulfilment decisions and specially helps when the demand is volatile. It also leads to smaller safety stocks at the stores. But it may also require more frequent and smaller shipments that affect the shipping and receiving operational costs.

Finally we will look at the supply chain processes, and how they get affected in each of the options.

Together this methodology provides a thorough decision support mechanism for selecting the optimal distribution models.

Lead-time and Inventory

Lead-time

We will assume that the lead-time in this context is the total time between the creation of demand at the store and its replenishment. From this point of view, the "warehouse" and the "cross-dock" models provide comparable lead-time efficiencies for the store.

However the "warehouse" model provides an inherent advantage. By maintaining the warehouse inventory, it helps in absorbing the variability in the demand and supply processes; and spares the stores from the effects of demand volatility.

The same is not quite true in the "cross-dock" model as there is no inventory to buffer such effects. Cross-docking models can distribute to stores using the original demand make-up, or by looking at the latest demand and re-allocating merchandise as it is received. While the latter provides a little respite by matching the latest demand against the supply, it still cannot address any system-wide demand surge, or drops.

The lead-time in "direct-to-store" delivery models gets adversely affected due to various factors. Among them are the mixed orders that suppliers need to fill to optimize transportation on a single store demand; locations of supplier warehouses; and the shipping lead-times.

Inventory

Inventories are required to be maintained either at the store, or at the warehouse, or at both the places.

In the "direct-to-store" delivery models, the inventories are required only at the stores. However the longer lead-time in this mode of replenishment requires that higher inventories be maintained at the stores for maintaining the desired service level.

In the "warehouse" model, the inventory is required largely at the warehouse with a small safety stock at the store. Low lead-times and guaranteed service levels; almost take out the need to maintain sizable safety stock in the stores. This is especially suitable for items with low or intermittent demand as centralized inventory in the warehouse provides optimal inventory deployment scenario.

In the "cross-dock" model, the inventories are likely to be lowest. There are no inventories at the cross-docking facility; and stores need to maintain just enough till the next delivery from the warehouse. The demand planning ordering cycles can be tuned to optimize the inventory requirements.

Supply Chain Processes

Demand Planning

We will define demand planning in this context as demand forecasting, inventory planning, and replenishment planning to produce the final need quantities.

In a "direct-to-store" model, the demand planning process is relatively straightforward. The historical sales at the stores are the clear demand stream that can be directly used for future projections. Also this is a single echelon supply chain model with no requirements for demand propagation, or time-phased planning.

The "warehouse" model primarily targets the replenishment at the warehouses. To calculate the demand at the warehouse, one can use the historical shipments to stores, transfer order requests from stores, or the actual store sales propagated and time-phased at the warehouse echelon of the supply chain. The last one is the most desirable, but also most expensive to model and compute.

The "cross-dock" model can actually combine the best of both worlds for demand planning. It allows the demand to be planned at the store level, but consolidates this demand at the warehouse level so that consolidated orders to the suppliers can be created. This adds some complexity to the process; and may also require that the original store demand be maintained for final disbursement of merchandise at the flow-through centre. Alternately dynamic allocations can be carried out at the time of receipt at the cross-docking facility.

Ordering

The process of ordering itself does not change much in the three scenarios. However the number of orders in the system varies widely. As each order incurs a processing cost, the higher number of orders to be processed can become overwhelming.

In a "direct-to-store" model, the purchase orders are created at the store level. This naturally results in a larger number of the purchase orders to be processed. In addition, the ordering constraints like order minimums can further make the process inefficient as the stores have to wait till they have enough demand to reach the order minimum, or artificially inflate the demand that may result into unwanted inventory. The upside though, is that there are no internal transfer orders to plan and execute as the orders are directly delivered at the store.

The "warehouse" model consolidates the store demand at the warehouse. As each warehouse may be fulfilling demand for several stores, it substantially reduces the number of orders to be managed. However there are internal transfer orders to be fulfilled that add to the costs.

The "cross-dock" model also consolidates the individual store demand to create aggregated orders for the suppliers. However this model requires that either the original store demand is retained for distributing the receipts, or an additional process of allocation is deployed to disburse the merchandise at the flow-through centre.

Logistics

There are considerable differences in the logistics processes in all the above scenarios.

The "direct-to-store" model can result in a large number of less than truckload "LTL" shipments. As orders are created for direct delivery to stores, the opportunity to consolidate orders to create truckload "TL" shipments gets reduced pushing up the transportation costs. However there are warehouse tasks of receiving, putting-away and fulfilment that get eliminated in this approach.

In the "warehouse" model, the inbound transportation can be greatly optimized through consolidation of orders, and shipments bound for the warehouse. However the warehouse adds its own layer of activities and costs, before the merchandise reaches its final destination at the store. These activities consist of receiving, disposition, put-away, storage, order-wave, picking, packing, staging, and shipping at the warehouse.

The "cross-dock" model provides the same inbound transportation optimization opportunities as above. However it does add some of the warehouse activities and costs. The flow-through requires the merchandise to be received, sometimes broken-up, staged, re-palletized and shipped. However it does save on put-away, storage, order-wave and picking activities at the warehouse.

Supply chain management is all about flows. Material flowing through warehouses is no exception. Conventionally the warehouses were set up as inventory buffer points along the supply paths so that demand fluctuations across the network could be smoothed. That provided stability to the planning and operations of the supply chain.

But better technology, integrated systems and near real-time information exchange have all made it possible now to operate the warehouses more efficiently. Where the product and demand attributes allow, it is possible to leverage cross-docking opportunities and reduce the inventory buffers at the warehouses.

Cross-docking basically involves receiving the merchandise at the inbound docks and then shipping it out shortly after without the need to stock it at the warehouse. If planned and executed properly it saves the intermediate disposition, storage and order fulfilment tasks in the warehouse. Well planned cross-docking operations save resources across the board, at the warehouse like labour, space, and equipment; and also technology resources by simplifying the process.

As cross-docking does not require the inventory to be stored at the warehouse, it provides dual advantages of:

1. Operational Efficiency: As the material does not have to be stored at the warehouse, and directly moves from the receiving docks to the shipping docks or staging areas, the warehouse operations are more efficient.

2. Inventory Efficiency: As the inventory moves directly from the receiving to shipping docks, there is no storage at the warehouses for the cross-docked items and that reduces the total system inventory in the supply chain.

There are two variants of cross-docking that can be leveraged. Both of these address different situations and need specific process/system capabilities but both are founded in the cross-docking concept and provide the same advantages.

Planned cross-docking or flow-through

Planned cross-docking is a deliberate strategy for the supply chain. It consists of determining the products that will be the best candidates for cross-docking/flow-through operations, and then deploying a complete demand and supply management process that leverages the flow-through strategy at the warehouse. These products will typically show the following characteristics.

Such products will normally have consistent demand that is not too high or too low. They can be seasonal as long as the seasonal demand has the same stable characteristics, and the processes can handle data specific procedures. The values of these attributes need to be established based on the sales history data, averages, and the speed of movement of specific merchandise. If the demand is too high then the items may be best served with a direct-to-store distribution model, and if the demand is too low/intermittent, then stocking at DCs may be required to consistently meet service levels.

They have good handling characteristics, through they can be conveyable or not. Flow through operations may require staging, pallet-breaking, and re-packing; and some product may just not have the physical characteristics conducive to that.

Once the target products have been determined, the implementation of the strategy requires that the supporting business processes are adjusted for making the shift. Some of these are discussed below in the section on pre-requisites.

Opportunistic cross-docking

This is an ad-hoc cross-docking process that takes advantage of real-time information exchanges among various distribution and fulfilment systems. Opportunistic cross-docking identifies when an inbound shipment or part of shipment (LPN/pallet) can be used to fulfil an outstanding order by directly routing the inbound merchandise to the staging or shipping docks for an outbound order. Opportunistic cross-docking is typically a pure cross-docking exercise and does not require any break-pallet or other similar intermediate tasks.

This type of cross-docking is not as process intrusive as the above. It is simpler to implement, and only requires that the warehouse systems have real-time visibility into all requirements, on-going shipping and receiving activities, and yard inventory; and that they can react to such information dynamically. This means that the warehouses are using the RF based devices and processes, rather than paper based processes.

Technically, most of the current systems are deployed in an integrated fashion, networked with other enterprise applications through messaging, and can exchange information in real-time; thus making this a reality. Therefore this largely becomes a business decision.

This type of cross-docking may also not provide any significant inventory reduction benefits but this is broadly applicable across most products, and provides the warehouse operation efficiencies without large changes in the business planning and execution processes.

Are you ready?

If you are ready to implement a flow-through strategy at the warehouses, make sure to review and plan through some of the following areas.

1. Warehouse Readiness: The physical assets in the warehouse, warehouse design, and layout affect the ability to implement a successful flow-through strategy.

2. Warehouses for cross-docking typically need large number of dock doors, and large areas devoted to staging. These warehouses can be seen to have two categories of products, "flow-through" and "stock-and-distribute". Depending on the proportion of the flow-through assortment compared to the total warehouse assortment, the areas required for staging, and the number of dock doors will vary.

3. Flexible yard management processes are another requirement before successfully deploying the flow-through strategy. The warehouse system should have visibility into the inventory in the yard, as well as enough yard jockeys to manage the trailers between the docks and the yard.

4. Mechanization can help. When large assortments at the warehouse are conveyable, mechanization helps simplify the flow of merchandise through the warehouse from the receiving docks to the staging areas, or shipping docks. This is not a pre-requisite but

can have huge cost impacts if planned properly.

5. Business Readiness: Flow-through processes require changes in existing business processes and expectations.

You will need to establish business processes and organization to identify and maintain the best candidates for flow-through. As described above, there are certain product, and demand characteristics that define such products. These characteristics can change over time (such as demand), and will require a review of the target assortment. You will need to establish the criteria, frequency, and ownership for these processes. The inventory profiles of these products will vary as they move to the flow-through strategy. It is important to understand how such changes will affect the current inventory metrics, and team's perception of success.

6. Replenishment planning is the other business process that impacts the flow-through strategy. The process must consider that there is no warehouse storage of these products any more. This may mean adjusting safety stocks at the stores, service level expectations, and potentially adjusting the frequency and size of orders. Some of these changes may need re-negotiating with the suppliers and may have their own lead-time.

7. Fulfilment network must be reviewed to make sure that all stores are within an acceptable distance from their primary distribution centre. Flow-through strategy may result in smaller but more frequent shipments to stores. Make sure that your distribution network is capable of handling such changes without adverse effect on the service levels.

8. Distribution processes get affected when the warehouse task planning reacts to real-time changes in receiving and shipment requests. Make sure that the people in the distribution centre and the stores are aware and have bought into the strategy. Consider things like fixed schedules and frequency of receiving in the stores, relative priority of shipments received from the DC over shipments from suppliers, store labour planning and scheduling models. All these processes may need to be reviewed and validated for their alignment with the new strategy.

9. System Readiness: Finally, your enterprise systems must be ready to support the changes in the business processes, and operations.

10. Analytics: Make sure that you have enough historical sales data and analytics capability to define the best targets for the flow-through strategy.

11. Warehouse Management: Warehouse management systems will typically need to be

integrated with the enterprise systems to receive real-time updates on shipments, material requests, and distribution orders. They should be able to react to these changes and re-plan if required. A paper based process in the warehouse cannot be used for changes in plans dynamically, make sure that the system supports the wireless handheld terminals in the warehouses. A warehousing system that is integrated with the automation/mechanization increases efficiencies, and reduces errors.

12. Forecasting and Replenishment: Review your forecasting replenishment processes to establish the level at which the forecasts and purchase orders are generated. Inventory planning systems that can dynamically compute the optimal inventory levels and guarantee service levels ensure a successful transition to the flow-through strategy. Collaborative orders and fulfilment environment with your suppliers can help. Inventory visibility across the enterprise across all inventory carrying locations is another useful tool to have. All these capabilities enhance the efficiency of the flow-through process, however only some of them are required and will hinder the implementation.

13. Allocation: A flow-through environment makes it possible to review the original allocations again at the time of receiving the

142

merchandise. Though it is not required, it allows the retailers to react to any demand changes in the time between when the order was placed and when the merchandise is received. The concept is very similar to manufacturing industries holding off the final assembly to the last possible minute. If you decide to re-allocate at receiving, make sure that the allocation systems are capable of reviewing and re-allocating merchandise on-demand. The alternative strategy also requires a review of the system to make sure that the order pegging is maintained between the DC and store orders.

14. Logistics: Flow-through implementation may affect the characteristics of the shipments from DC to stores. You may have more number of shipments, more multi-stop shipments, and more frequent shipments. Make sure the transportation systems can optimize such shipments, track them as they move, and allow changes by the users if required.

Cross-docking or flow-through is definitely a strategy worth a serious review. However a successful implementation requires that the people fully grasp the concept, and plan vigorously for success.

Chapter 25: Growing Economies around the World and Supply Chain

This is based on the premise that the world as a whole is evolving in all possible aspects politically, financially, socially, and culturally. While all these aspects of this evolution are important the one we are most interested in evaluating is the economic aspects of this evolution. Growing economies around the world affect how the corporate supply chains will emerge and grow with it. It affects all aspects of the supply chains including sourcing, purchasing, suppliers, logistics, assortments, and selling.

As economies grow, so does the consumption. The new demand-supply equation affects the costs till the equilibrium is reached again. This change in costs and their management is one the trends that I believe will affect the supply chains directly.

The two largest components of costs for retailers are the cost of purchase, and the cost of distribution. Right now both of them are trending up, as they have done for most part of this year and the last year. While supply chains have always focused on costs, and cost savings through more efficient planning and operations has been their core value proposition till now, supply chain costs have been evaluated in isolation. I believe that is about to change. Pioneers will start looking at a more holistic picture of cost of "doing business" rather than focusing on specific supply chain areas such as logistics. This broader view of the costs will cause evolution of processes that go across merchandising, supply chain and sales; and would provide a common sense of cost and profitability to the corporations of tomorrow.

While these changes could be driven from various points of view, driving them from the supply chain point of view may be most logical as the discipline already provides a framework for modelling costs, networks, processes and leverages mathematical optimization.

The Rising Costs of "doing business"

We mentioned above that the two largest components of costs for Retailers are the cost of merchandise, and cost of distribution. Cost of distribution is easier to understand as it is largely related to warehousing and transportation. The rising cost of energy has kept the focus sharp and clears on this part of the cost equation. The other cost, namely the cost of merchandise is the one that is defined in very narrow terms today, and needs to be expanded and evaluated with sharper focus.

Most corporations with advanced supply chain teams focus on both of these costs through optimizing various supply chains functions such as Sourcing, Inventory Planning, Replenishment Planning, Warehousing and Transportation. The current processes, however evaluate these costs in silos and even when optimized, the models do not provide any global evaluation of these costs or any ability to compare scenarios and predict long term effect of decisions.

I believe that this is the next big opportunity for cost savings. The continuing pressure on costs with a weak economy and resulting inability to pass on costs to consumers are going to drive the companies to evolve these processes further to squeeze as much cost from their eco-systems as possible. Today there is almost no visibility or understanding of the "total costs" of the merchandise and in fact, most retailers lack the information, inclination and the capacity to do this.

To provide a better context, we will borrow from the concept of "customer life-time value" (CLV). The objective of determining the life-time value of a customer is to focus on long term customer service/satisfaction for an overall higher profit from the relationship, rather than maximizing short-term sales revenues. And putting such programs actually work.

Total Life-time Cost

So what is the "total life-time costs" of a product? The question may not sound as interesting as CLV though it is a pertinent question to ask. The life-time costs of a product will include not only the cost of purchase, but cost of planning the assortment, planning the demand, sourcing and evaluating the suppliers, actual purchase costs over the whole season or life of the product, cost of distribution, cost of marketing, cost of mark-downs, cost of returns, cost of customer relationships due to gaps in the customer expectations and product functions, etc. This is what I call the "total life-time cost" picture for the merchandise and it is this picture that will be enabled by the processes of the new supply chains. It is this picture that will then become the basis for product portfolio and profitability analysis that should ideally drive the assortment decisions for the retailers in future.

Let us again go back to the "cost of distribution" for a minute. This has attracted and retained put attention not because it is the largest part of the cost in the equation but simply because it is easier to measure and control. Most companies can track what they pay to their carriers, and how much it cost them to run their warehousing operations. Anything that is easily understood and measured gets our attention. Even though the "actual" cost of distribution for a specific merchandise is debatable due to crude cost-allocation practices, we at least know the total costs across the enterprise related to distribution.

Now let us look at the "cost of merchandise". Is this the cost that is paid to the suppliers against the purchase orders? What about the cost of creating and processing the purchase orders? What about the cost of planning the replenishments? What about cost of inventory planning that determines the final replenishment numbers? What about the cost comparisons among suppliers that have contracts with price-breaks going over a few seasons, and affect the total costs over the life of the product? What about the cost of signing a contract that goes bad and needs re-negotiating or legal action? What about cost fluctuations due to currency variations for merchandise bought foreign suppliers, and transported by foreign carriers? What about customer returns, mark-downs, marketing, cost of bad assortment decisions, etc, etc.

There are just too many pieces to this cost that are very fuzzily defined in today's cost accounting processes, and therefore fail to provide any sense of "what does it really cost me". These processes need to be defined better and tied together in the definition of "cost of merchandise" so that a merchant can actually make decisions that are objective and based on data rather than instinct and experience.

Understanding these costs will affect almost all processes; the way we assess the product profitability, assortments, sourcing, replenishment strategies, inventory policies and of course the logistics.

New View of the World

Another aspect of life that changes for supply chain strategist as a result of the "rise of the rest" is the procurement strategy. For almost two decades now, China has been the focus for cheap manufactured goods. Prior to that it was Japan. Cost equation simply worked that way. The depressed wages, cheaper energy prices, an abundance of labour, and almost non-existent middle class to drive local consumption all of these factors favoured China to be the manufacturing hub of the world.

Almost all these factors have changed in recent years with consistent trends. Wages in China have doubled, energy prices have quadrupled, commodity prices have almost doubled, and China's middle class has emerged as a substantial "consumer" in its own right.

The changes in each of these factors will cause changes in the procurement strategies. These changes will make the cost equation more equitable, and allow more regions of the world to participate in global commerce. What that means to the supply chain strategist is that the supply chains will grow to many more regions of the world, bringing in more complexity in ocean routes, port management, trade terms, compliance, foreign currency planning, cultural factors, financing and settlement. The increased complexity then will cause companies to re-evaluate the tools of the trade and invest in applications that help them address and grow with the new set of supply rules.

The Integrated View of Costs

Now imagine a hypothetical application that actually can project all the cost components mentioned above over the useful life-cycle of a product. And think how this will change the process of evaluating and launching a product. Also think about how such a process will have an integrated view of the currently siloed processes of product life-cycle management, merchandising and supply chains. You might shorten a season just a week to reduce the cost of mark-downs; you might split your purchases just so to optimize your seasonal ramp-down efforts in northeast that start a few weeks prior to ramping-down in south-east; you could just predict the total cost of merchandise procurement over the whole season because you know your projected demand at various nodes and command suppliers to use preferred warehouses for supplies; you could buy a week ahead to avoid the projected currency exchange rates that favour your supplier.....and so on.

Jog your imagination and see for yourself the possibilities of the future supply chain strategies and decide how to evolve to that next level.

Chapter 26: Transportation Operations Effectiveness

Transportation operations are a big part of a retailer's distribution functions. These costs can be up to 20-30% of the total supply chain costs. Transportation costs have been brought back into focus with the cost of fuel as it is a large part of the overall transportation costs.

Managing the transportation operations will help manage the costs better. But what exactly do you manage? An old cliché – you can't improve what you can't measure. So what do you measure to manage the transportation operations?

One of the difficulties in defining these metrics is that most companies define a more generalized set of metrics for distribution, and this generalization takes away the focus from transportation operations and dilutes it with metrics that measures warehouse operations, fulfilment rates, inventory efficiency, etc. While it is completely sensible to measure these metrics to keep a healthy distribution system humming along, the specific metrics mentioned below are more sharply focused on measuring the efficiency of transportation operations, and controlling costs.

To obtain the transportation efficiencies and reduce the costs, the emphasis should be on creating better loads, reducing miles through better route planning and route optimization, optimized carrier selection, and finally validating what you pay for freight.

Build Better Loads

How many of your loads are TL "Truck load" versus LTL "Less than truckload"? What is the average capacity utilization of trucks or rail-cars or containers for each of the road/rail/ocean modes? You can measure these by some of the following indicators. If you are carrying too many LTL loads, there may be opportunities for consolidation and creating TL loads. If the average utilization is low, then you can improve on load-building, and review your ti-hi requirements and compliance to these requirements. "TI-HI, or Ti-High refers to the number of boxes/cartons stored on a layer, or tier, (the TI) and the number of layers high that these will be stacked on the pallet (the HI). It can also be used in reference to the stacking pattern used to load a pallet in order to generate a relatively stable stack".

Also keep an eye on the trending for these metrics as that can be a predictor of the efficiency of overall transportation operations.

1. Number of loads that were TL, LTL from the total number of loads.
2. Average truck/container utilization that can be measured by calculating the total freight (weight and volume) carried during a time period divided by the total capacity (weight and volume) of the equipment used for the purpose.

Reduce Miles through Optimized Routes

Measure average number of miles for a ton of freight in your distribution system. For any given period of time, consolidate all tonnage carried, and all miles travelled. Divide latter by the former and study the trend. Are you driving more miles to deliver a ton of freight, or less? As companies grow so do their freight tonnage. But using better software to optimize the loads and routes, better efficiencies can be achieved so that this ratio does not have to grow in the same proportion.

1. Total miles travelled
2. Total tonnage carried
3. Average number of miles travelled per unit weight of freight

Optimize Carrier Selection

Review your carrier selection during the transportation planning. How many carriers do you have in each mode? Do you have enough volume leverage for each mode? Are there lanes that are not covered by any carrier contracts? How does the carrier selection algorithm work for the shipments? Some of the metrics that can help you measure the efficiency of carrier selection process is as under.

1. Total number of carriers used by mode in a period.
2. Total load carried by each carrier versus number of shipments.
3. Total number of shipments carried with carriers with a contract versus general carriers.

4. Total freight carried with carriers with a contract versus general carriers.

Validate what You Pay

Finally do you have a process in place that allows you to validate the freight invoices? Does your process allow you to estimate the cost of freight against the carrier invoice? What about the accessorial costs? Do you have a lot of claims? Some of the following metrics may be useful.

1. Accuracy of freight invoices, as invoices that were validated and found to be correct versus not.
2. Freight invoice auto-approval, as invoices that were validated by the system and approved versus those that needed manual touch for any reason.
3. Average cost of shipment per unit. If the freight units are a combination of multiple units of measurement, you may normalize this as the cost of a ton-mile of freight.
4. Average cost of inbound freight (calculate same way as above).
5. Average cost of outbound freight.
6. Total freight as percentage of COGS, further split by inbound freight and outbound freight costs.
7. Total accessorial cost as percentage of total freight, same ratio for inbound and outbound freight.
8. Total claims as a percentage of total freight costs.

Chapter 27: Transportation Management Systems

Companies are reporting lower revised estimates citing higher energy costs. Higher merchandising costs, and higher freight costs were among the culprits identified.

Higher fuel and energy costs seem to be one of the single largest factors affecting the upward cost spiral for retailers. The energy used in manufacturing processes cannot be reduced very quickly as any changes in manufacturing process reconfiguration are bound to have large capital and time outlays. The second largest energy cost is in the transportation. We estimate that transportation costs can amount to 20-30% of the total supply chain costs.

Transportation Optimization/Management Systems can help you in many ways to address the rising cost of freight. Deploying these systems is not a quick fix, but they have a proven ROI, and have even better return in current times with fuel spiralling upwards steadily.

Transportation Management Systems (TMS) can yield substantial results through reduction of miles, optimal load and long-haul profiles (shifting of LTL loads to more TL loads), increased use of multi-modal shipments to better utilize the transportation network, and finally by reducing the freight cost invoicing errors.

Load and Route Optimization: Reduce Miles, Enhance Long-haul Legs, Increase Cube Utilization

TMS applications create better loads, allowing more efficient use of the trailer, rail-car and container capacity. They can also plan better routes to create multi-stop routes, continuous moves, and by utilizing pool-points where such trans-shipments may reduce the cost of freight. These systems also have the ability to create multi-leg, multi-modal shipments that can leverage cheaper transportation modes. For example using rail for the long haul portion of the route, and road for the final delivery leg can substantially lower the cost of transportation. Line haul rates for rail and ocean (where that makes sense) are much more favourable compared to road freight.

While the inter-modal transportation always adds some more process complexity, the TMS applications make this transition easier by allowing you to automate most of the interactions between the carriers, drayage services, and the warehouses. On-boarding the partners, and certifying such automated interaction will still pose a challenge, but the rewards more than pay for such an initiative.

Freight Invoice Audit: Look before you pay

TMS applications also typically help in auditing the carrier invoices by validating shipments, line-haul, and accessorial charges. These not only make sure that the freight invoices are paid only for the services, but also ensure that the freight is being calculated using the contractual rates, and that all the accessorial are valid. It also prevents overpayments to carriers thus avoiding collection fees to 3rd party debt collectors when carriers fail to respond to the debit notes.

Fleet Management: Enhance Utilization, Reduce Miles

Most distribution intensive business use dedicated or own fleets for delivery to their stores. TMS can help enhance the fleet utilization efficiency for dedicated fleets by reducing the fleet miles travelled through better route planning. This is primarily obtained through multi-stop routes while simultaneously constraining on the warehouse shipping and store receiving schedules. Every mile saved on the fleet not only saves on the direct fuel cost, but also increases the fleet life due to associated wear and tear.

Chapter 28: Transportation versus Inventory

In talking to a senior executive from a supply chain solutions company I heard an interesting comment that more and more companies are looking at transportation optimization in the face of rising fuel costs. Of course there is a direct link between rising costs, and the desire to do something about it, but it also got me thinking about what other factors may be driving the interest in transportation optimization.

Traditionally the inventory has been the biggest focal point for supply chain managers. That makes sense as inventory consumes a substantial amount of operating cash flow for retailers. Assuming an inventory turns value of 7 for example, a retailer with $10B in revenues would have locked almost $1.5B of operating cash flow in the inventory. Therefore any reduction in the inventory results in more money available to other functions. However that is a double edged sword; achieve overly enthusiastic reduction in inventory and you will lose sales (and hence revenues) due to stock-outs, but under achievement results in bloated inventory that will eventually require clearance and pull down the margins.

Finding that golden "optimal" level that balances the two sides (service and excess) is hard to establish and harder to maintain as demand patterns evolve and change. Inventory joins the demand with supply and it is this inherent position that makes it dependent on the supply and demand planning processes. In fact this dependence is very critical. The accuracy, stability and consistency of demand and supply planning processes affect the efficacy of the inventory planning. And that directly impacts the inventory levels and ability to service demand. Inventory planning typically uses demand, supply and lead-time for determining the optimal inventory levels to maintain a specific service level.

All the above makes it almost necessary to review these processes together to have any appreciable impact on the inventories. The combined impact of demand planning, inventory optimization, and supply planning processes can result in huge savings through reduced inventory in the system, lower clearance costs and better financial efficiencies. However it is a large effort and it impacts a large number of users in an enterprise. It also requires good clean master data and large amounts of historical transactional data, both of which need additional effort to obtain. This generally makes it a little more complex and requires a clear consistent strategy to successfully deploy. The rewards are bigger, but so is the effort leading up to it.

Let us also examine how the savings in inventory affect the company financials.

Inventories exist as assets (current assets to be specific) on the balance sheet. Any reduction in inventories therefore reduces the total assets and impacts the asset turnover ratio. A higher asset turnover ratio basically means that the corporation is able to generate the same revenue by deploying fewer assets than before. Assuming all else remains same, it results into higher ROA (return on assets) that can do wonderful things for a corporation like raise its share price, enable it to pay higher dividends, ability to expand or do any of the other things that spare change can do. Reduced inventories also reduce the inventory carrying costs (hence COGS), but the impact is relatively small because the fixed costs remain the same and only variable costs are reduced.

The financial impact largely makes the corporation more efficient in using the available resources.

Transportation

Compared to the inventory optimization, transportation is a different story. It is almost an opportunity for the taking. No matter how the replenishment was decided, eventually what has been ordered needs to be moved from the suppliers to the retailer's warehouses, and from then on to the stores.

The transportation optimization just does not depend on other processes like the inventory optimization does. And almost all the data that this solution needs such as routes, rates, lanes, carriers, purchase orders, and weights/volumes of items is deterministic and largely available in the enterprise already. The only exception to this required data may be the volumetric and weights for the items but that too can be obtained in collaboration with suppliers. For an average retailer, shipping costs used to add up to 1.5 to 3% of the revenues (that is, when the oil was still not trading in the stratosphere, it would reasonably be higher now). Assuming a 2% rate, it is still a cool $200M for a $10B retailer. And unlike the inventory savings that indirectly improves ROA; any savings in transportation are immediately visible to the bottom line.

Here is the financial side of the story

Shipping costs reduce the cost (hence COGS, cost of goods sold). With all else remaining same, it directly impacts the profitability or margin. First and foremost, profitability directly shows up in the bottom line, and provides extra cash for any other priorities. Then improved margin also improves the ROA and allows the companies to do all the wonderful things we mentioned above that can be done with spare change.

Finally it looks like addressing inventory improves overall health but requires a broader approach to reviewing the business processes involved in supply and demand planning, but addressing freight costs is a quick solution to a specific problem of runaway fuel costs. And just as fortifying your diet with vitamins will make you stronger and healthier; an impending infection can only be cured with a strong dose of antibiotics. For now, inventory looks more like the vitamins while transportation is the strong dose of antibiotics. Take your pick!

Chapter 29: Replenishment Policies and Inventory Planning

The two processes of replenishment and inventory are closely related. The inventory planning process establishes the optimal inventory levels that must be maintained to meet expected service levels for demand fulfilment. What does that exactly mean? To understand we need to explore the replenishment (or re-ordering) process. In doing so, we will also establish the decision parameters an inventory planning process provides for the replenishment to work at its most optimal levels.

Replenishment or Reordering

Reordering or replenishment process needs to define review period for reordering, and an ordering quantity. Then it needs the inventory parameters to determine whether an order for replenishment should be placed at the time of review or not. Based on how the review period and order quantities are defined, there are a few options to drive the reordering.

Continuous Review and Periodic Review

These terms refer to the frequency of review to determine when orders must be placed for replenishment.

In the continuous review process, the inventory levels are continuously reviewed, and as soon as the stocks

165

fall below a pre-determined level (usually called, reorder point, or reorder level), replenishment order is placed. As more and more companies start using sophisticated IT systems to track their inventories in real-time, the continuous review method becomes a viable and optimal way to plan for replenishment.

Under periodic review, the inventory levels are reviewed at a set frequency. At the time of review, if the stock levels are below the pre-determined level, then an order for replenishment is placed, otherwise it is ignored till the next cycle. This method provides a viable process alternative to the continuous review by segmenting the merchandise into review buckets. This makes it easier to manage when the process is manual, or the number of items involved is extremely large, or when constraints on ordering-day exist.

Order Quantity and Order up-to Level

These terms refer to the process that is used to determine how much is ordered when a replenishment order is placed.

In the first process, the "order quantity" is fixed. If the review determines that an order should be placed, then the order for a pre-defined quantity for that item-location combination is placed for replenishment. The order quantity for all replenishment orders is fixed in this method, though order day may vary or may be fixed depending on the review method.

The second process defines a pre-determined "order up-to level" instead. The actual order quantity is determined as the difference between the on-hand stock on the review day, and the pre-determined "order up-to level". The order quantity in this process will differ from one order to another depending on the on-hand quantity on the day of the review.

Between these two sets of parameters, four basic reordering process options become available.

Options for Re-ordering Process

Based on the above two parameters, the reordering process can be deployed in the four basic ways.

Inventory Planning

The two key inputs to optimally run the reordering processes above are the inventory safety stock and reorder levels. These parameters control two of the most critical factors in a supply chain, the amount of inventory, and the ability to maintain favourable service levels.

And both of these are defined by the inventory planning process. As the demand and supply patterns change, the optimal inventory levels required to guarantee image desirable service levels also change.

Due to inherent variability in the demand and supply streams at any supply chain node, the ability to service demand directly depends on the safety stock. The relationship between the two is exponential that means that a 100% guarantee to fulfil demand will, in

167

theory, require an infinite amount of safety stock to be maintained.

A good inventory planning process helps define these levels, discriminating between products that require higher service levels versus those that don't. It helps in maintaining user defined service levels that guarantee desirable fill-rates to fulfil the demand. It also reviews them frequently to make changes to the safety stock recommendations to adjust to the new demand/supply picture.

Here is a quick synopsis of the inventory planning or optimization process that determines the optimal inventory levels to meet a desired service level.

Inputs to Inventory Optimization

The inventory planning process takes the following inputs.

1. Desired Service Level: this is normally a user provided input. The desired service level depends on the item in question, its sales attributes, demand, profitability and associative relationship to the other items. Users normally define groups of items that have similar attributes to define and manage the service levels.

2. Demand: this is the historical and projected demand for the item at the location. Note that the demand at a location like store will be the POS (point of sale) history, while demand at a distribution centre is simply the requests that stores placed on the DC. If the store requests

on the DC are not available, one could use the outbound shipments as an approximation of such demand.

3. Supply: this is the historical and projected supply of the item at the location. The supply at a location like store will be the shipments history from DC, and/or vendors; and supply at a distribution centre is generally the inbound shipments from vendors.

4. Supply Lead-time: this is the historical lead-time of the supplies. The lead-time may vary for every PO/transfer order that is fulfilled even for the same item/vendor/distribution centre combinations. This time-series data provides the variability of such lead-time and helps the inventory optimization engine to determine the probability that a specific projected supply will be realized on the need date. Image.

Process of Inventory Optimization

The inventory planning process determines the variability of the historic data to determine the optimal inventory levels. Most algorithms use statistical methods, and are therefore computationally intensive.

The process pre-processes the time-series data for demand, supplies, and supply lead-time to compute the mean and standard deviation of these series.

It then computes the optimal inventory levels (safety stocks) that will be enough to guarantee the target service levels.

Outputs of the Inventory Optimization
The process can recommend the following decision parameters that are then the inputs to the reordering process itself.

1. Recommended safety stock levels.
2. Reorder levels,
3. OUTL (order up-to levels), and
4. Order quantities for the fixed order quantity scenarios above.

Chapter 30: Maintaining a High Level of Service and Low Costs

The balancing act of maintaining a high level of service and low costs is becoming harder for retail supply chain directors as businesses try to meet the growing customer mantra of "more for less." This pressure comes at a time when business is becoming more global, supply chains are lengthening, and competition is on the rise.

Although this challenge is not new, the outlook is that it will intensify as a number of factors; economic, regulatory and market-driven become more acute. Consequently, supply chain performance will have increasingly significant impact on overall business success.

Globally, forward-thinking retailers are also redefining the way they do business with their customers and their suppliers, adopting innovative ideas to respond to market trends and developing new channels to meet consumer shopping preferences, many of which are being brought about by shifting lifestyles in Western economies.

Already highly complex, the supply chain of the future will grow even more complex as it serves a greater variety of buying channels (store, Internet, kiosk, telephone, mail order, TV, PC) delivering to more outlets (different store formats, order and collection options, homes, multiple pickup options) in potentially more regions all while managing more products from a greater number of sourcing locations.

Although the supply pipeline needs to be more efficiently designed so that goods can flow seamlessly from the producer to the consumer, it will also need to work well in reverse to release value tied up in returned and obsolete products; and it will need to do so as quickly as possible at the lowest possible cost. This issue will become more critical for European retailers required to comply with the European Community (EC) legislation dealing with product disposal (Directive on Waste, Electrical and Electronic Equipment) and existing laws on traceability and product recalls.

In addition, companies are looking at ways to provide a more proactive service and to ensure that the supply chain does not collapse in the "last 50 yards." That is because, while retailers have invested heavily in supply chain initiatives, the supply network itself has not benefited from information technology as much as other parts of the enterprise. However, retailers are trying to better balance supply and demand (with a strong focus on demand intelligence and forecasting analytics to better plan business from supplier to shelf) and acknowledge that the introduction of more appropriate technology could improve overall consumer satisfaction within an environment of rising operational costs.

Although technology alone is not the answer, when combined with changes in business processes and business culture, it can go a long way toward delivering "more for less." Influences on Technology Implementation Given the pressures to keep costs low and service high, most retailers will choose to make supply chain modifications rather than fall victim to increased competition. Whether they undertake large-scale restructuring, small, incremental improvement, or something in between, there are a number of factors that can affect any technology implementation.

Supply Chain Visibility and Control

Supply chain directors need to maintain end-to-end visibility and management of the supply chain, either by taking greater ownership through centralized distribution or by working with a few closely integrated supply chain partners to achieve the desired results.

Third-Party Integration

Many retailers rely on the services of third-party logistics companies to deliver specialized services. Given the additional integration and coordination requirements, this can slow down the restructuring process.

Loss of the Big Picture

As more companies look at ways to provide more proactive service and reduce costs, supply chain directors may try to focus their attention on specific points within the supply chain, resulting in "point solutions" or software for specific tasks such as store task management, transport scheduling or merchandising management, resulting in the inability to see the bigger picture and need for integration.

Understanding Costs

It has never been more important to understand true supply chain costs that can affect trade-off decision making. This often requires data to be captured and analyzed in completely new ways.

Technology Confusion

Many retailers recognize technology as an enabler, but it can also be considered a hindrance. Today, there are more technology choices than ever, but not all are accompanied by clear business benefits. This creates a high degree of scepticism and uncertainty from supply chain professionals. It is important for companies to educate themselves on new technologies to better understand their opportunities.

Accuracy and Visibility

One key investment retailers are likely to make is in areas that will help improve visibility of products in the supply chain and allow real-time, accurate information to be easily accessed and shared collaboratively with all parties within the chain. In particular, retailers will look for ways to streamline product introductions, make ordering and replenishment processes more effective, and analyze data that will show what consumers will want to buy in the future, enabling better category planning.

Tracking with Radio Frequency Identification

Radio frequency identification (RFID) tags are evolving as a major technology to track goods and assets within the retail supply chain. There are already a number of global retailers using RFID-enabled tags on pallets, cartons and even individual items. RFID tags can carry more information than a bar code and can be scanned without line of sight by a high-speed reader from a distance of several meters. Readers are being used in distribution centres, at store receiving bays and at doors to the shop floor, enabling retailers to compile and analyze data about in-store and on-floor stock levels and goods in transit with point-of-sale data. Early results of the Wal-Mart RFID initiative have shown a reduction of 16 percent in out-of-stocks. Because RFID is still in its infancy, many retailers aren't sure when and how to utilize the technology. Many retailers are waiting for a compelling business case, adopting a pragmatic attitude, and hoping that norms and standards will stabilize before pushing for adoption. However, since industry-driven standards for the use of RFID are becoming more prevalent, retailers are increasingly looking at where the benefits of using RFID might be in their own business model (such as the ability to find stock quickly or count it faster), while keeping up-to date on how the technology is being developed and deployed.

A first step should be to more fully understand its potential use and then to identify the gaps in current capabilities that might be improved by RFID usage. A more pressing concern may be to simply make better use of existing information.

Chapter 31: Connecting Strategy to Supply Chain

Going from business strategy development to creating tangible competitive advantages is a long journey. Because no strategy, however brilliant, produces results unless executed.

Therefore, to be useful, a strategy must be implemented. This means that the strategy that establishes the business goals, through which competitive advantage will be created, must then be expanded to articulate actions that will take the business toward its strategic goals. This whole process can be thought of as consisting of three basic steps:

1. Strategy development

That is, the process of evaluating the internal and external imperatives, analyzing the industry, products, and customers, and defining an overriding principle of how the company will try to grow. This is equivalent to defining the "what" and "why" of the problem.

2. Strategy planning

Is the process of assessing the current state of the corporation and evaluating various alternatives that can be potentially considered to achieve the stated imperatives of the business strategy. This step consists of analysis, evaluation, articulation, and prioritization of these alternatives, in effect defining the "how" of the problem.

3. Strategy implementation

Is the process of starting and managing the individual projects to implement the favoured alternative from step two. While most companies have some level of formally defined process for developing a business strategy (step 1) and an ongoing slew of projects (step 3) creating new capabilities and enhancing existing ones, most do not have a formal process for the activities identified in the strategy planning step.

We recognized this gap because the planning phase focus on gap-assessment of a firm's business capabilities, therefore determining what must be done, strategy execution emphasizes the actual execution activities; program management, project management, change management, communication, training, and all other organizational aspects for successful execution. While that is important, the intermediate analysis provided by strategy planning is the missing link in most modern corporations in any recognizable formal fashion. In absence of this planning step, corporations fail to establish and prioritize the execution efforts that are aligned with the goals of the business strategy, and fail to identify and prioritize the filling of specific capability gaps.

This middle step of strategy planning is what we call functional strategy. This is the step where firms must assess their business capabilities and determine (1) what capabilities they must build that are aligned to their business strategy and (2) how they must build them to create differentiators to create competitive advantage. This is where the business functions such as supply chain fit-in. This is where a firm needs to assess their current and required supply-chain capabilities to identify the gaps and prioritize their investments in building those missing capabilities.

Joining the business strategy to the functional strategy by assessing your supply-chain capabilities is the key to building successful supply chains. The final piece of execution is what we call deployment strategy falls into place when real projects enabling specific process are planned, budgeted, spun off, and executed. Understanding this continuum from the business strategy to functional to deployment is key to successfully creating competitive advantages to support your business objectives.

Chapter 32: Managing Suppliers Process Compliance

It is a cliché but it is still true. You don't know what you don't measure, and you can't improve it either. Retailers need to maintain their service levels, they need to make sure that the shelves are adequately stocked with the right merchandise when customers come looking for it. This is no small job, given the large assortments, complex replenishment processes, and a large number of suppliers.

Suppliers (used in a generic sense including merchandise suppliers and carriers, alike) play a huge role in smooth operations of a Retailer especially in the execution phase. They affect what gets shipped, where, how much, when and in some cases, how. While there is a mutual expectation for compliance to Retailer's requirements, it may not always happen. Unless of course, if retailers measure their suppliers for good execution performance and process compliance.

Here is a quick primer on what to measure for effective supplier relationship that compliments your business goals rather than hurting you.

Fulfilment Execution Metrics

Fulfilment execution measures how effectively the suppliers fulfil the merchandise orders. The process efficiency revolves around the three main factors, Quantity, Quality, and Time.

Quantity

This metric primarily provides the fulfilment rates. There are various quantities that could be measured for effectively measuring the order fulfilment process. These are Ordered v. Confirmed; Confirmed v. Shipped; Shipped v. Received; Shipped v. Invoiced; and finally a Fill Rate calculation that makes sense for a Retailer. Most relevant definition will be to compare the Ordered Quantity to Received Quantity. Order quantity comparisons mentioned above (if routinely short of expectation) simply point to the sub-process that may be under optimized and needs attention. A Perfect Order metric is usually a composite metric generated from the above as orders that were fulfilled on-time, complete, damage-free, and accurately invoiced. However there is no single definition of perfect order and this metric can be computed based on what makes the most sense for a retailer.

Quality

Most Retailers do not require inspection on inbound merchandise. However the quality matters. It affects Retailers' operations through increased consumer returns, unsatisfied customers, and additional labour to process returns. Retailers can get a good grasp on quality by measuring Damaged Packages, Damaged Goods, and Customer Returns. The first two can be made part of the warehouse standard operating procedure "SOP". Visually check damaged packaging at receiving, and flag the transaction. Check for damaged goods when pallets are broken into case/boxes. Customer returns are captured through the store returns process or RMA generated/received for the other channels.

Time

This is third metric for measuring the effectiveness of the fulfilment process. There are two types of metrics for time that should be tracked.

1. First one of them is the lead-time. There are various types of lead-times that are important. The total fulfilment lead-time consists of lead-time components that are controlled together by the supplier, and the carrier. Some of these components are the Order Acknowledgment Lead Time (time between the order transmission date, and order acknowledge receipt); Order Processing Lead Time (time between order transmission date and RTS (ready-to-ship, typically EDI document, request for routing); Ready to Ship Confirmation Lead Time (time between receiving a request, and sending back a, routing instructions document); and finally the Transportation Transit Time (time between pick-up shipment status message, and yard-check-in at the destination facility). Keeping tabs at the lead-time provides realistic data for replenishment systems that helps create correct demand forecasts. Trends in lead-time usually point to a broken sub-process.

2. The second one relates to the activity level SLA (service level agreements). Examples in this category are violations of pick-up and delivery-time windows by the carriers.

Once these metrics are measured, they can also be shared with the suppliers as a score-card. Retailers can use them to identify the top and bottom suppliers to prioritize their relationships.

And finally, Retailers can charge-back when suppliers fail to live up to contracted service levels.

The second part of effectively managing supplier relationships is process compliance. In this part, we cover the Process Compliance Metrics for the supplier performance management.

Well established processes normally provide a repeatable performance that is efficient, normally highly automated, and does not depend on individual level of skills to achieve a dependable result. Purchasing processes cross the organizational boundaries and their total efficacy depends on how well the suppliers comply with the Retailer's processes. Measuring process compliance helps Retailers identify the suppliers with issues, and address these issues before they start affecting the supply chain efficiency.

The key to a successful process compliance program is to identify which transactions are core to the smooth functioning of the purchasing and delivery processes. Within these transactions, it requires that the key data elements are identified clearly. And finally it requires that these expectations are plainly defined and become part of partner contracts. These transactions cover the merchandise suppliers, as well as carriers, and can consist of all the following.

1. Vendor facing: Purchase Order Acknowledgement, Request for Routing Instructions, ASN (advanced shipping notice), and Merchandise Invoices.
2. Carrier facing: Load Tender Response, SSM (shipment status message), and Freight Invoices.

Having these transactions automated (for example through EDI messages) helps in capturing when the process breaks as well as managing the resolution quickly.

Process compliance metrics normally measure the following three aspects of any transaction:

1. SLA (Service Level Agreement) Compliance: It measures whether a required transaction response was sent within the agreed time. For example, if PO Acknowledgements are expected for every PO within 24 hours of transmission, then this metric will track how many POs did not get any acknowledgements, and how many acknowledgements were received after the required 24 hours SLA. It applies to all the transactions mentioned above, but is required to be measured only if it brings specific value to the Retailer. For example, if PO Acknowledgements are used to project on-order quantities and enable

order promising, it will be a good transaction to track. However if no other functionality depends on this transaction, there is no need to require or track this SLA.

2. Format Compliance: This measures if the required transaction has any format issues that may have caused the transaction to fail. Most relevant for electronic transaction exchange (EDI/XML/pre-formatted files), it ensures that the automation does not fail and transactions are not dropped unexpectedly through the process due to formatting errors. For example, if dates are required to be transmitted in mmddyyyy format, was it done? For EDI formats, did it have all the required segments, and was the format of each data element as expected?

3. Content Quality Compliance: It measures the data quality of the transactions exchanged. For example, if the ASN must reference the PO number then this metric will measure how many ASNs (advanced shipping notice) did not have the PO number (this filed was left blank), and how many had an invalid PO reference. Of course this requires that such fields are clearly identified and communicated to the partners in advance.

Just like Fulfilment Execution Metrics, these metrics can also be shared with the suppliers as a score-card. These can also be used to identify the top and bottom complying partners to prioritize the efforts of the compliance teams. And finally, Retailers can charge-back when suppliers fail to live up to contracted process compliance agreements.

Chapter 33: Supply Chain Environmental Consciousness

Environmental Consciousness primarily focuses on the changes happening in today's manufacturing, and distribution industries in response to the enhanced awareness of the impact of these activities on the environment.

While this trend has been in the making for some time, it has gained great momentum in the recent years. The rising awareness of the impact of the human activity on the environment is the subject of discussion in more and more political, social and economic forums. It is also the subject of numerous reports from World Bank's Environmental Sustainability to Human Development Report 2007/2008 from United Nations.

Manufacturing and Distribution are two activities that affect the environment on a large scale. Manufacturing needs raw materials that come from natural resources in a number of cases, and the manufacturing process invariably needs energy to convert these raw materials into the finished products. Along the way it may produce wastes that must be treated, if toxic, before it can be released back into the environment. Distribution needs energy to move the products from one place to another and is a direct contributor to green house gases and resulting warming. Supply chains manage manufacturing and distribution processes. And that is what brings them into sharp focus from this point of view.

While there are not many regulatory requirements that constrain the supply chain processes directly at this time, the indicators suggest that such requirements will exist pretty soon. Carbon emissions trading are already a reality in EU, and there is active talk of this system as a mechanism to control and govern the environmental effects of the industrial activities in the US as well. (Note that the US has operated cap-and-trade systems for emissions of sulphur dioxide and nitrogen oxides for year now). Both of the above systems, namely the carbon labelling as well as the trade-and-cap systems can directly contribute towards controlling the environmental effects of manufacturing and retailing activities. Both affect the supply chain functions and its future evolution. The first achieves it through direct consumer discrimination based on the consciousness and the second one achieves it through regulation that affects the competitiveness of enterprises that are less environmental friendly than others.

While some of these measures will be voluntary and others regulatory in nature, it is clear that such measures will effectively change how we as consumers behave and react to products we buy. For example, consider the nutrition labels that were required to show the Nutrition Facts, basic per-serving nutritional information, on foods under the Nutrition Labelling and Education Act of 1990. These were introduced in 1992, and since then it has become an important part of the consumer behaviour. It is not uncommon to find people checking the nutrition information in the grocery stores prior to putting the merchandise in their carts. A similar concept for carbon labelling will undoubtedly affect consumer behaviour, and hence the retailer's behaviour in how these products are assorted, sourced, processed, distributed and sold.

Carbon Labelling

California's Carbon Labelling Act of 2008 proposes to "Establish a methodology for determining and communicating the carbon footprint of a consumer product. If feasible, the state board shall establish standards and methodologies for determining and communicating to consumers on a product label whether a product has a lower carbon footprint than the average comparable product available in the state."

Chances are that such a methodology will include some measure of

1. Energy consumed in the production of a product, and disposal of any harmful by-products.
2. Energy consumed in the distribution of a product from the manufacturer to the retailer's facilities, and finally.
3. Recycling characteristics of the materials used in production.

Most of this information can be collected from the manufacturer and the retailer, and standardized in a format that is easy to understand and discriminate.

191

And such labels will in turn affect the consumer preferences that drive the merchandising, sourcing, purchasing, distribution and stocking processes.

Trade-and-cap

The trade-and-cap system will primarily affect the manufacturing costs and affect the overall price paid by the consumer. Environmentally unfriendly products, even if cheap, will still have some impact in the same way as the allegations of using child labour had in recent years. This combination of regulatory and voluntary pressures will affect the consumer behaviour albeit in a slightly indirect manner than the carbon labels. Managing costs eventually affects the same supply chain processes as above; merchandising, sourcing, purchasing, distribution and stocking.

The decision parameters and the metrics that define and measure these processes will change in response to these changes. So far these were primarily back-end supply chain processes that were merely enabling getting the right product at the right place at the right time and quantity. In the new context, they become front and centre processes whose decisions affect the ultimate profitability and success of the company.

Chapter 34: Supplier Performance Measurement and Compliance Management

Supplier performance measurement and compliance management go together. Both of these solutions feed from the same data as the supply chain visibility. However the business ownership for the supply chain visibility normally resides with the operations team, while the vendor relationship organization owns the supplier performance scorecards, and compliance. Given this organizational dichotomy, many organizations tend to pursue separate solutions for these two related capabilities. From the solutions point of view, though it is most desirable to pursue a single solution that addresses these needs together.

Three types of solution providers can address such needs...

VAN Providers

These are the VAN (Value Added Network) providers that normally provide the EDI services. In the past few years though, most of the VAN providers have added application functionality to their services that enable visibility across the chain. For supply chain operations, such visibility goes across the purchasing, shipping, distribution, and receiving and settlement functions.

Most of these functions use standard EDI communications. Some very common examples being 850/855/860/856 for purchase orders and ASN; 204/990/214/314 for load tenders and shipping; 110/210/810/820 for invoices and remittance.

As these transactions pass through the VAN, these providers have built applications and reporting to provide the supply chain visibility, vendor performance and compliance metrics. Organizations may need to feed some additional data for receipts as that is generally an internal transaction and may not go through a VAN provider's network.

All of the major providers in this space provide such capabilities. Most of these vendors also provide charge-back capabilities for non-compliant vendors; pro-active notifications; and web-portal for score-cards as well as dispute settlement are some of the other nice features to consider.

The advantage of this approach is that no extra data interfaces need to be built, and there is very little IT effort involved in standing up this capability once the business metrics have been established. A web-portal is generally part of the solution and on-boarding is provided as an additional service if desired.

The solutions in most cases can be hosted, or brought in-house; or purchased as extended services to VAN, or exclusive of VAN services. Costs must be considered for all the services desired.

ERP Vendors

Next class of solutions in this space comes from the standard ERP vendors. All major ERP vendors cover the functionality as part of their SRM (supplier relationship management) suites. SRM supplier management function collates all the required data from purchasing, receiving, transportation and warehousing modules of the ERP to create and provide the scorecards. Any charge-backs as a result of non-compliance are sent back to the ERP's finance modules.

Consider this solution approach if an ERP is already in place, and most of the related supply chain functions have been deployed preferably on a single vendor solution. This option may turn out to be more cost-effective in these cases.

Niche Vendors

Then there are vendors that specialize in this functional area. These are dedicated vendors that provide extended solutions and services in the space. They have well-packaged out of box solutions and can help in situations where business requirements are not well understood, or not yet matured. Consider them to bring on-board the business expertise needed to set up such programs and for a quick packaged solution with well defined footprint.

Chapter 35: Trends that Will Define Future Supply Chain Strategies

The sands of supply chain strategy planning are shifting again. It has evolved a lot, and changed a lot; and, it is happening again. The imperatives driving the supply chain for the next few years are becoming visible and they will shape this phase of supply chain evolution.

Supply chain was MRP in the 80s, that evolved to constrained based planning in the 90s, giving way to an integrated view of planning and execution currently through corporate-wide visibility and rich analytics.

Still so far, only a handful of companies have treated supply chains as a core part of their corporate strategy. These corporations have seen ample rewards in doing so. But most others had just started to seriously consider investments in supply chain strategy, when the new ground rules seem to be emerging for the next generation of supply chain thinking.

In making these statements, I want to differentiate between the automation of supply chain execution versus a truly strategic thinking that reviews the corporate supply chain from a strategic point of view that drives business functions and decisions.

The automation of supply chain transactions simply provides for efficient operations. Its value lies in the productivity enhancements that such systems provide. The business transactions in this category are largely standard, unvaried, and are supported through a multitude of vendor solutions available for all budgets. A good example in this category is warehouse management systems. While they do have a good ROI, these systems do not necessarily provide any competitive edge. These systems are no more elite, but have rather migrated into the "required" category if you wish to do business.

The strategic view of the supply chain attempts to view the corporate supply chain as a business strategy that binds together the assortment, sourcing, demand and supply management, planning and operations as a "whole" rather than the sum of its parts (like managing a warehouse). This is where the visionary corporations are focused and should be investing. This is what drives Wal-Mart to review Brazil as a major market, GE to invest in the middle-east, and Halliburton to move their HQ to Dubai.

And it is the latter (strategic view of the supply chain) that is going to undergo major transformation in the coming years as corporations adjust to the environmental changes underway for the last year or so.

We will talk about the two overbearing trends that are driving this change. In the next two chapters, we will go into the details of these trends and the shape of things to come.

Merchandise Costs: "Rise of the Rest"

At the core of this trend is the fact that living standards are rising all around the world. The developing countries are growing at a faster pace than ever. And the combination of growth and higher living standards is pushing the wages and cost of production specifically in these regions, and generally all over the world. People have argued that this growth is also pushing the prices of food, commodities, and energy everywhere.

This trend affects the cost basis for everything that is manufactured and distributed, through the increased cost of materials, cost of higher wages, and finally the cost of transportation. The changes in the cost basis will change the outsourcing equation in manufacturing.

The commodities index for all commodities has gone up by 44% from 1998 to 2008 (Source: Bureau of Labour Statistics, Jan 1998 versus Jan 2008). Over the same time period, the index for Metals and Metal Products moved up 65% and Industrial Commodities by 45%. All the indices were still trending upwards for 2008 at the time of writing.

The wages in China have nearly doubled in past four years outpacing the growth of GDP. According to the Department of Energy, the cost of diesel fuel has almost quadrupled in the same time from 1998 to 2008.

These changes are not isolated spikes in a stable data series anymore. These changes have become trends that will define the cost equations for the decades to come. And these new cost bases will define the sources of our goods and services in the next few years. The change may not be subtle, China may not be manufacturing capital of the world any more, and India may not remain the back-end services capital. Consider some of the recent changes on manufacturing front; BMW starting a manufacturing plant in the US, Inbev buying Anheuser Busch and Chinese investments in manufacturing coming to GA facilitated by the Georgia China Alliance.

Business Costs: Environmental Evolution

The second trend that will shape the supply chains of the future is the environmental awareness, and the social pressure to address the issues related to the environment. This can manifest itself through various legal and regulatory requirements, such as the carbon trading; or in more stringent ways that affect the whole chain of raw materials, manufacturing processes, disposal and recycling. There is talk of "carbon labelling" in the industry that would require the retailers not only to gather the information but also share it with the consumers. These changes, legislative and otherwise, will drive the companies to review their existing processes and enhance them to align with the changes in the external environment.

These changes in the environmental sensitivities have the potential of affecting almost all of the organizational supply chain processes. Some of the processes directly impacted will be assortment planning, sourcing, vendor selection, manufacturing processes, packaging, disposal, distribution.

Over the next two chapters we will dig deeper to find out how these two trends affect the supply chain strategy and planning for the corporations.

Chapter 36: Make People Part of Your Equation on Supply Chain Technology

As awareness around supply chain functions has grown, so has the software applications available to address these functions. In fact the supply chain has been among the most expanded solution area for ERP companies during the last decade.

However, unlike the transaction processing ERP systems, the supply chain functions tend to provide a decision support tool that can be complex. Consider demand forecasting, inventory planning, replenishment planning, transportation planning, bid optimization; these are all areas that actually provide the users with modelling, evaluation, and analysis tools for real-life scenarios rather than simply automating transaction processing. Therefore, these and other supply chain solutions routinely utilize techniques such as statistics, time series analysis, linear programming, mixed integer programming, dynamic programming, decision trees, probability, queues, data mining and so on.

Putting the power of real science to work behind these solutions improves the solution quality, and allows these solutions to model real-life scenarios closely, consider a large number of parameters that may affect the results, and leverage ever expanding computing capabilities to provide solutions within minutes making close to real-time changes possible.

But it also increases the complexity of these solutions, and requires that companies employ people with the right skills who are capable of using such solutions through training, academic background, or both. And that is where most companies appear to lose all their commonsensical ability to judge the value of their investments. There are far too many implementations where the businesses have chosen to spend millions on the best of breed solutions but then pulled back when it came to invest in quality of people who would be using these solutions and actually make possible the solution ROI. No wonder ROI on software solutions has always been questionable even though real results can be achieved with some common sense.

Suppose you spent a few millions buying a jet, you would most certainly invest in an experienced jet pilot, rather than trying to teach your chauffeur on how to fly that plane. Almost all large corporations own their private fleet of jets these days, and the pilots and other crew to go with these planes always without question.

Now consider the same corporation investing the same few millions on a high-end demand forecasting system that utilizes sophisticated statistical forecasting techniques, and requires a few people with doctorate or masters in statistics to set up the system, tune the forecasting parameters, review the forecasting errors/trends from time to time to ensure that the system is running at its very best and providing good forecasting projections. While most of the users of this system could be people with average academic and professional experience, but a few of the super users controlling and tuning the system had to be statisticians. Suppose also that the solution vendor is naïve enough to mention this during the sales pitch, where do you think it would go? Chances are such an open admission of skills required to run the system will not go down well, and such naïveté will cost the solution provider the business.

How many times have you heard the refrain that if the system requires a PhD to be run, then that is a problem. But the fact is that some systems are complex, and they do need highly skilled people to run them, tune them, and keep them in good shape. And just like the example with the jet above, these systems do pay back in terms of saved time, increased data accuracies, objective decision support, scenario playing and other similar capabilities that are impossible to achieve manually, or by using systems that don't quite provide the capabilities to keep them simple.

On the other hand, not everyone may need a jet either. Therefore evaluate your needs clearly, and if you do need a system with all the power of science and mathematics behind it, go for it, but also remember to plan the right people and skill-set to go with that!

Chapter 37: Conclusion

Supply chain practitioners have emerged as a vital partner in the most strategic aspects of managing complex, global companies. In years past, the procurement function (the sourcing of essential products and services on the best possible terms) occupied centre stage. But more recently, the relentless focus on driving out costs has taken a backseat to such issues as supply market risk, revenue enhancement and managing complex supplier relationships.

A Strategic Perspective

During my days as Operations Director, I have always expect our head of sourcing and materials management to provide a strategic perspective on the markets we deal with, identify and mitigate supply-related risks, lead change internally and work with our supply base to identify and contribute their best ideas. That means contributing to the major areas that drive value creation; revenue enhancement, cost reductions across all areas of spending, working capital improvements and better capital project development and execution.

Many complex problems that resist solution respond when framed as supply chain management issues. Hospital medication errors, for example, are responsible for more than 400,000 preventable drug-related injuries each year, according to the Institute of Medicine of the National Academies. It's tempting to think of the hospital medication errors crisis as a problem for Doctors and Nurses to solve. After all, it's doctors who prescribe and nurses who dispense the medication.

The physician community tried and failed to conceptualize a solution to this issue. The solution, now rapidly being implemented at hospitals, flowed out of decision to frame the problem as a supply chain management opportunity.

Managing Complex Customer Relationships

Supply chain management should no longer be focused solely on driving out costs. When it is aligned with the business priorities of the organization, supply chain management can play a fundamental role enabling the company's growth agenda, mitigating risk and delivering competitive advantage across the end-to-end value chain.

Although identifying and driving out costs will always remain part of the mix for organizations with mature supply chains, the reality is that there is relatively little incremental cost available for cutting as markets mature, the real opportunities for SCM (supply chain management) are in identifying opportunities for revenue enhancement and helping the CEO manage increasingly complex customer relationships," Dearth says. "Visionary CEOs see profit opportunities in taking a holistic, end-to-end approach that integrates procurement teams across the business."

Consider the increasing complexity of customer relationships faced by the CEO of a company. Given the relatively small number of major players in say the chemical industry, companies often finds themselves negotiating with a company that is at once a supplier, a customer and a competitor. It's a fine balance that can be easily upended by a procurement manager so narrowly focused on shaving a few cents off the price of a commodity that the customer relationship becomes strained, It's so easy to get into contentious relationships with partners when there are overlapping interactions. A good Supply chain practitioner will apply just the right amount of pressure on pricing so that it doesn't disrupt strategic supplier or customer relationships.

Here's a cautionary tale of what can go wrong when procurement goes for a quick win without considering the larger picture. The procurement manager of a $40 million technology company demanded new payment terms of net 60 days from all of its suppliers. Good for the company's cash flow, right? Not really. At least one supplier was also a large customer that purchased more product from the company than it sold. That supplier/customer, in turn, demanded 60-day terms from the technology company. Result: a net disadvantage.

Where a supply chain practitioner really earns his or her seat at the table is partnering with the CEO to optimize capital allocation, increase return on invested capital and reduce total costs of ownership. If that sounds like the CFO's job, welcome to the brave new world of SCM.

209

Good Luck!

Resource and References

Drucker, P. (1993) Post-Capitalist Society

Drucker, P., "What Makes an Effective Executive", Harvard Business review, June 2004

Lessons from Toyota's long drive, an interview with Katsuaki Watanabe, HBR, July 2007

Liker, J. & D. Meier, Toyota Talent, McGraw Hill, 2007

Shook, J. , Managing To Learn, Lean Enterprise Institute 2008

Fishman, C., "No Satisfaction", Fast Company, Dec 2006/Jan 2007

Womack, J. & J. Shook, Lean Management and The Role of Lean Leadership, Lean Enterprise Institute presentation, Oct. 2006